Aspergirls

by the same author

22 Things a Woman with Asperger's Syndrome Wants Her Partner to Know
Rudy Simone
Foreword by Tony Attwood
ISBN 978 1 84905 883 4
eISBN 978 0 85700 586 1

22 Things a Woman Must Know If She Loves a Man with Asperger's Syndrome
Rudy Simone
Foreword by Maxine Aston
ISBN 978 1 84905 803 2
eISBN 978 1 84642 945 3

of related interest

The Growing Up Guide for Girls
What Girls on the Autism Spectrum Need to Know!
Davida Hartman
Illustrated by Margaret Anne Suggs
ISBN 978 1 84905 574 1
eISBN 978 1 78450 038 2

Girls Growing Up on the Autism Spectrum
What Parents and Professionals Should Know About the Pre-Teen and Teenage Years
Shana Nichols
With Gina Marie Moravcik and Samara Pulver Tetenbaum
ISBN 978 1 84310 855 9
eISBN 978 1 84642 885 2

Safety Skills for Asperger Women
How to Save a Perfectly Good Female Life
Liane Holliday Willey
Foreword by Tony Attwood
ISBN 978 1 84905 836 0
eISBN 978 0 85700 327 0

Aspergirls

Empowering Females
with Asperger Syndrome

RUDY SIMONE

FOREWORD BY LIANE HOLLIDAY WILLEY

Jessica Kingsley *Publishers*
London and Philadelphia

First published in 2010
by Jessica Kingsley Publishers
73 Collier Street
London N1 9BE, UK
and
400 Market Street, Suite 400
Philadelphia, PA 19106, USA

www.jkp.com

Library of Congress Cataloging in Publication Data
A CIP catalog record for this book is available from the Library of Congress

British Library Cataloguing in Publication Data
A CIP catalogue record for this book is available from the British Library

ISBN 978 1 84905 826 1
eISBN 978 0 85700 289 1

Printed and bound in Great Britain

MIX
Paper from
responsible sources
FSC
www.fsc.org   FSC® C013056

To Mike W.

Who gave me a different lens to look through

ACKNOWLEDGMENT

I would like to sincerely thank the women who participated in the making of this book, as well as their partners and parents. I was honored by your trust, and I hope I've done it justice.

CONTENTS

ADDITIONAL TOOLS FOR PARENTS

APPENDIX

FOREWORD

I was not diagnosed with Asperger syndrome (AS) until my daughter was diagnosed. This was almost fifteen years ago. At the time, few people I knew had even heard of pervasive developmental disorders, much less AS. Happily, much has changed since then. These days, I would imagine virtually everyone remotely interested in human behavior or current events has heard of Hans Asperger and his "autistic like" patients who struggled with non-verbal communication skills, peer interaction, limited but intense interests (and yet, higher than average IQs), strong verbal skills and an awesome ability to recall details and facts. Asperger syndrome is a media darling which shows up everywhere from the red carpet of Hollywood to the smallest school district's special education discussions. Google the term—you'll see what I mean. While it is stirring for those of us with AS to see all of this attention being focused in our direction, many of us remain without a formal diagnosis, particularly if we don't have a Y chromosome. Females, from the littlest of girls to the eldest of ladies, continue to fly under the radar of proper diagnosis, eventually landing in worlds where they don't belong. Neuroses, schizophrenia, obsessive-compulsive disorder, personality disorder, oppositional defiant disorder, anxiety issues, social phobia—these are familiar diagnoses for women beyond a certain age who struggle to make sense of the environment, society, relationship rituals and the like. Not that these diagnoses are completely off base. The chances are very good that any mix of those comorbid factors also lay on a lady's genetic code. The problem is many counselors and doctors seem unable to see AS crouching in the middle of the huddle. Why then (many of us ask) does a diagnosis of AS remain a guy's thing? Why do researchers still report that AS affects males three to four times more often than it does females, despite top psychologists in the field, such as Tony Attwood, Judith Gould and Lorna Wing, trying to reframe our thinking from "AS does not affect females" to "how can we recognize AS in females?" I tend to think part of the reason is straightforward enough. Many women with AS are leery about coming forward with the suspicion they may be an Aspie because, as much as many of us like to say it isn't so, a diagnosis of any kind brings with it a heap of stereotypes and prejudice. Simply put, it is downright difficult to tell the world you are a square peg jamming yourself into society's round hole.

I am in awe every time a woman on the spectrum shares her experiences. I am indebted. And I am relieved to know that each day, more and more Aspie women are joining web forums, small group discussions, and friendship circles, to share advice on how to navigate the neurotypical world map. A voice here or there might not be heard, but the collective voice of women willing and able to share—wow. That's a loud chorus that can't and won't be ignored. Rudy Simone's book, *Aspergirls: Empowering Females with Asperger Syndrome*, has a lead role in that chorus, and will serve as an important catalyst to encourage contemporary thinkers to have the realization that a significant number of females do, in fact, have AS.

Simone's book is part memoir, part research review, and part user's guide to AS. The writing style flows smoothly from the page, making it an eloquent, yet relaxed and informal, and always very informative, read for anyone interested in life outside the box of normal. Couple this with Simone's fresh and spot-on voice perfectly capable of expressing what life with Asperger syndrome is often about for women on the spectrum, and you have a superb read on your hands. Superb reads are great for the mind, but essential for souls hoping to move toward an understanding of things new, things different and things worth cherishing.

I identified with just about everything in this book. Page after page brought me closer to my own feelings as I highlighted sentences and earmarked pages to share with others. I was especially touched when I read the personal vignettes which Simone includes. People on the spectrum often say they appreciate and deeply respect the experts in the field, but no one can tell it like it is better than those who walk the spectrum walk. All the women who shared their experiences for this book are doing more than walking the walk. Their insight is invaluable to the community. Simone does an excellent job of incorporating others' words with her thoughts, and then rounds everything up with practical advice for growing and enjoying life.

Simone coins a new word in her book—"Aspergirls" is what Ms. Simone calls women with AS. I like it. My daughter said the term sounds like a superhero. Fine by me, and, I suspect, fine by Ms. Simone. I don't think anyone could read this book and not come to the conclusion that women who manage to come through the gauntlet of AS with any measure of success are indeed super *and* heroes. But like every hero, women with AS are bound to be susceptible to some sort of Kryptonite. Simone takes on these poisons one by one. Bullying, self-esteem, anxiety attacks, melt-downs, sex, guilt…the list goes on, but never without supportive insight aimed at assisting the downward falls with a myriad of suggestions and positive images that will refuel the reader's desire to get up and carry on with one's head held high and one's spirit moving in a comfortable direction.

New books are always exciting, but only a certain few have staying power. *Aspergirls: Empowering Females with Asperger Syndrome* is here to stay.

Liane Holliday Willey, EdD
Author of Pretending to be Normal: Living with Asperger's Syndrome, Asperger Syndrome in the Family: Redefining Normal, *and editor of* Asperger Syndrome in Adolescence: Living With the Ups, the Downs and Things in Between

INTRODUCTION

Women on the spectrum are a subculture within a subculture. We have many of the same quirks, challenges, habits, traits and outlooks as men, but with our own twist. It is not so much that Asperger syndrome (AS) *presents* differently in girls and women, but that it is *perceived* differently, and therefore is often not recognized.

When I read the words of other Aspergirls such as Liane Holliday Willey, Donna Williams or Mary Newport, I get incredibly excited, because now I finally recognize myself in other women. This is something I was *never* able to do before; I have never identified with my female classmates, peers, and certainly not with media representations of what a female is and should be. I also do not relate to the media images of autistic children who are far more obviously challenged than I ever was. This is the crux of AS—our challenges are very real but not always obvious to others. Therefore our behavior is not understood.

It is sometimes said that every person with Asperger's has some form of savant skill. Mine seems to be, if I have one, seeing patterns and threads connecting disparate concepts. While some of the topics in this book might seem a little random to a non-spectrum person at first, Aspergirls reading this book will understand. These are the issues that affect most if not all of us; the ties that bind us.

Some of the more obvious and talked about side effects of AS are things like depression, sensory issues, difficulty with employment and cultivating relationships. But there are other things that comprised my life experience and shaped my character and I wanted to see if other Aspergirls had similar views. I asked questions like:

- Do sensory issues affect your choice of partner?

- Do you like sex?

- What do you think of gender roles?

- Motherhood?

- Do you feel any guilt because of AS?

- What causes your meltdowns and what does the process feel like? Can you stop them before they start?

- How many misdiagnoses did you receive before Asperger's was finally hit upon?

These are some of the things that have sculpted my life in a way that other observers might not think to ask about or document, but I feel they are intrinsic to having Asperger's and being female. Men may share most of our traits, but I think that their way of experiencing and manifesting them is different. For example, we all know that men with Asperger's like to dress comfortably and may shop at thrift stores to get that broken-in feel. But in the case of women, the same trait often shows up as dressing like a teen, sporting little or no makeup and having a simple hairstyle. While people with AS may share a kind of androgyny, this appears in AS men as a gentleness; Aspergirls have a tendency to be independent and wield power tools.

This book is needed because of the subtle difference between the genders on the spectrum, but also to address the differences between an Aspergirl and a non-spectrum female, otherwise known as an NT or neurotypical girl. We may have similar goals, but the nonautistic, by capability, devotes more of herself to a wider social circle. The Aspergirl, by necessity and exclusion, if not by choice, has more time to devote to her inner life and to her goals. But we are not more likely to reach our goals because we don't have the social skills which are usually the requisite means to pull us up the ladder of success in our chosen field.

For the Aspergirl, everything seems to be about purpose and reason, which we don't always find in the trappings of this noisy, chaotic, confusing world. So we create our own world in which to do our own thing, and so live isolated lives, never engaging as fully with others as perhaps we could or we want to. The trade off to this hermit-like existence and many hours spent focused on work or hobbies, is that we may become cynical and closed off to the beauty of life…and to companionship. What I believe is that Aspergirls are a subculture; what I promote is a cultural exchange: To teach spectrum girls how to engage a bit more with others so that our lives reach their maximum potential. In return, the non-spectrum population has to understand that the Aspergirl has much to offer; that her depth and her talents should be prized; her eccentricities and quirks tolerated if not wholeheartedly accepted.

At the time of this writing, approximately 1 in 100 children are on the autism spectrum. How many adults, we'll never know, but surely it is more than previously thought, because Asperger's simply hasn't been understood enough to be recognized. Males are believed to outnumber females four to one although experts like Tony Attwood are calling into question that official ratio. I believe that Aspergirls may be as plentiful as males, we are just harder to spot. Not every one who is autistic is diagnosed when they are a child. But many women would *never* be diagnosed if they didn't have children on the spectrum. Then the physician may look to the parents to find the genetic source.

There are two accepted reasons for the rise in numbers:

1. A refining of diagnostic methods.

2. An actual rise in the number of people on the spectrum.

I propose a third:

3. The high stress life of the modern world, coupled with an emphasis on a person's social confidence, has made those of us on the spectrum feel our differences more keenly. This has caused us to seek answers—via the internet and books—leading to diagnosis.

To find out you're autistic is quite a realization to have in your teens, but in your 40s or 50s it means you have to look back at your whole life and re-frame everything; every incident, every moment, with this new lens to look through. It's like getting glasses after spending your whole life near-sighted. Obviously, the longer you've gone without the diagnosis the more work you have to do in looking back. And in some cases, the more damage to your spirit, psyche, and relationships you have to undo.

There are stages we have to get through once we, as adults of any age, find out we have Asperger's:

- *Awareness:* We find out about Asperger's and the information speaks to us but hasn't hit home yet. We might experience some resistance or denial.

- *Knowing:* The irreversible understanding that you have Asperger's. The realization clicks.

- *Validation:* Asperger's explains so much in a life that often seems to have had no rhyme nor reason. This is not one moment but a series of moments that will continue for years if not forever.

- *Relief:* I can finally, as the song says, "lay my burden down." We don't know what our burden is until we're diagnosed but we can tell other people don't seem to be carrying it.

- *Worry:* What does this mean for my future and for my potential?

- *Anger:* For all the blame and misdiagnoses that may have been laid upon us by ourselves or others. Hopefully we then get the next phase of our lives—

- *Acceptance/thriving:* We become keenly aware of our gifts and deficits and use what we have wisely.

What happens after diagnosis? How do we come to the place where we are thriving with Asperger's? The Aspergirls I've spoken with get most of their strength and information from the Asperger community, particularly forums, but that still comprises mostly males. There seem to be far more questions than answers on female forums. Asper*girls* have their own unique set of questions and attributes and very few resources to turn to.

My first high hope for this book is to help other Aspergirls feel validated; to be de-stigmatized if not esteemed. There has been a shift toward AS pride already; I am by no means the first to say "AS is a gift." My second is to help Aspergirls defeat depression; what I've learned is that it is our greatest adversary. Although it fuels our passions it also sabotages our efforts. What's so difficult to deal with is that it is an invisible, stealthy enemy—it sneaks up on us, blindsides us and kidnaps our time and energy.

My third high hope is to help professionals learn to spot the signs of AS in women. To stop in its tracks, and preferably before it starts, the long, tedious, unproductive pattern of misdiagnosis. Misdiagnoses have wasted a lot of time and energy on both our parts and have resulted, at our end, in a lack of trust in the medical profession, particularly general practitioners and mental health professionals.

Counselors, psychologists, doctors, and educators are trying their level best to get their collective heads around Asperger's, and offer valuable therapies and tools we can use. They have a bit more catching up to do where female AS is concerned. If you are an Aspergirl, you are a true authority on the subject. For this book, I consulted mainly females on the spectrum and a few perceptive mothers. I interviewed mostly high-functioning women in their 20s, 30s, 40s, and 50s. Only one teen was involved. This book will address the situations and aspects of AS that we contend with daily and will illuminate our various ways of coping. I hope we will learn from each other, and help the helpers in the process.

1

Imagination, Self-taught Reading and Savant Skills, and Unusual Interests

It is known that people with Asperger syndrome love information, but why? Information gives our thoughts an anchor, it gives us an identity and is something we can control. We don't have to charm it, take it to lunch, or impress it. It is ours to do with what we will.

We have a voracious appetite for it. We don't want to wait for kindergarten for the words on the page to reveal their meaning. We also don't want to wait for our first lesson to evoke music from the magical instrument standing in the corner. And often, we don't have to.

> I learned how to read from "Sing Along with Mitch Miller" records. One day I picked up *The Cat in the Hat* and I could read the words, they just suddenly made sense. (Widders)

My own process of learning to read was logical and quick. I remember asking my mother to show me the alphabet, and since "A was for apple and B was for boy," etc., I learned the sounds of the letters. By the time she finished going over the alphabet minutes later, I picked up a book and I was off. Most of the Aspergirls I interviewed were self-taught readers and many had similar experiences with maths, music, and design.

> I'm a spatial-mechanical savant. I have CAD (computer-aided design) for a brain. I can build electronics and machines from scratch with no background. (Andi)

This skill levels off as we get older. I believe that this early ability to read and comprehend above our years (hyperlexia) gives some young Aspergirls an air of intellectual maturity that tricks people into thinking we possess emotional maturity as well. It also hides autism by shielding our deficits.

Some Aspergirls are less language-oriented and, of course, some of us do possess learning disabilities such as dyslexia. But verbal or visual, learning difficulties or not, throughout our lives, much of what we want to know will be self-taught, even if we attend college. We like to teach ourselves just about anything we're interested in, not only because of impatience but also because we have our own methods for ingesting and comprehending. We might not "get it" from other's instructions, particularly verbal ones, and we take information in, in our own way.

> Almost everything I know is self-taught. I was a very fast learner at school but had low exam grades due to dyslexia so I was written off. I have taught myself statistics, chemistry, sewing, embroidery, and welding. (Sam)

Some people, like author Bill Stillman (2006), believe that children with autism have a "God connection"—that their deficits are compensated by a higher spiritual awareness which gives them access to knowledge and gifts. Experts tell me that people with AS have a higher-than-average IQ…yet we don't always project practical intelligence. When we're young we may be called "little professors," but when we get a bit older, we're more like "absent-minded professors." What has been lately proven, is that children with Asperger's have a higher rate of *fluid intelligence* than nonautistic children (Hayashi *et al.* 2008). Fluid intelligence is the ability to see order in confusion, to draw inferences and understand the relationships of seemingly unrelated things. While we may not have higher *crystallized intelligence* (the ability to use acquired knowledge and skills), this may explain why we sometimes just "know" how to do something, like solve complex maths before we are taught, or build electronic gadgets.

> I can fix or reproduce things, including devices and clothing, after just looking. (Dame Kev)

I do not mean to say that we are all blindingly smart; if you are an Aspergirl without any "zone passion," and you have no savant skill, you are not alone.

> What really makes me uncomfortable is when Aspie campaigners couch that "leave us alone" argument in the myth that *all* AS people are super intelligent mathematician science savants and some sort of master race. That makes me feel, as an Aspie who doesn't have any of that, I'm a double fail—I fail at being normal, and also fail at being AS. (Polly)

But those who fall into the slow learner category may do so for any number of reasons—from sensory processing difficulties; shutting down under pressure or around others. Dyslexia, dyspraxia and selective mutism can all play a role in making a smart girl be misinterpreted.

> I lived in my own sweet little bubble. I ignored most of what was going on around me. I couldn't read out loud (selective mutism), so the teachers all assumed I couldn't read at all. They wanted me to read low level books, but they were really boring, so I had to sneak upper level

books in the classroom and library. I got into trouble if caught with one of my contraband books. (Widders)

I was not in special ed but they always assumed I was stupid. I always had to prove myself and was frequently invisible. (Ann Marie)

Not comprehending things the way other people do is fine in academia because we can usually find our own methods, but in social situations, this same tendency plays out differently—we can't always impose our own rules and priorities on others. We can't research people in everyday conversation the way we research information from books. It is not uncommon for us, when we're young, to ask too many questions of others, which makes them uncomfortable. If we could set the tone, we would probably be more comfortable, but we can't so we shut down. This becomes most noticeable in the teenage years when conformity begins to be of the utmost importance. (We'll talk more about this in Chapter 9.)

It is often said that those with Asperger's have little imagination and do not engage in imaginative play as children. I think this is erroneous and may be a hindrance to identifying those with Asperger's who do possess a vivid imagination. Just because we like to arrange crayons by color or alphabetize our toys doesn't mean we don't want to use them. But the stories I made up in my head were far more interesting than the ones I could enact with my dolls—rigid, unconvincing bits of plastic.

The diagnosed Aspergirls I interviewed have varying degrees of creativity and imagination, from "none" to "extremely vivid." We all seem to start out by copying what we admire and some will stop there, at being great emulators.

I can remember music from beginning to end after hearing it only once or twice. I started violin at age five and played entirely by ear for years. If my teacher played the piece I was supposed to learn, I could play it back to her and just had to refine the technique. (Heather)

Put a pencil in my hand and I turn into the human copy machine. (Bramble)

Others have created their own works of note.

Orchestral pieces of mine were being played by people all over Europe when I was only 14. (Kylli)

My painting skills are completely self-taught. Everything I have learned is a consequence of personal research and self-directed study and reading. That is all I do. (Camilla Connolly, Australian artist and Winner of the 2009 Waverley Art Prize)

Another reason that autism may be overlooked is that our obsessions do usually fall under the heading of "normal" girlhood things, like books, music, art, and animals. It is the rapacity with which we enjoy them and the passion they inspire in us which is taken to a new level. While it took me a few years to begin to write original stories, songs, and essays, I read as if my very life depended upon it. I would fake being sick so that I could stay home and read. I'd bring snacks into my room in the morning because I knew I would not want to stop and take any breaks for food. I would have peed in my room if I could, just to not have to stop reading.

Why do we read with greed? (Or play, or design, etc.?) We want to fill our minds with knowledge the way others want to fill their bellies with food. Information replaces confusion, which many of us experience in interactions with others. It is a place to focus, apart from all the external stimuli in our homes, schools, shops, etc. It is completely within our control how much we want to let in, unlike dealing with people, who are unpredictable and uncontrollable. (Even those of us who are in our own bubble, who don't read or seem to look outward much, may have a rich internal world and not yet have such a need to connect.)

Information fills a void as we don't seem to have much of an identity of our own when we're young. We feel a sense of urgency to learn and create and you can't really create anything until you've taken in enough understanding of what already exists. In *Thinking in Pictures*, Temple Grandin (2006) says she learned how to draw engineering designs by copying another draftsman's drawings. She soon began to create her own highly complex works without any formal training.

Obsessive activity is an illustration of the incredible focus that we possess, and teachers, doctors and educators are beginning to realize this is an asset—something to be cultivated and not discouraged. As Temple says, we have to work with our strengths not our deficits. This is a key to the kinds of workers and innovators we might be in our future. But there are practicalities to attend to. When we are in *the zone*, we do have a hard time with taking breaks, going to the toilet, eating, drinking, grooming, getting fresh air, or exercise. It can also impinge upon getting a job, going to work, and other crucial activities. Is it really just executive dysfunction causing this behavior—not knowing when to stop? Or is there something more?

> It is the only time I experience a unified sense of self. Nothing else matters. (Camilla)

> When engaged in my passion I lose all sense that there is anyone else on the planet or that time is passing. It is like another dimension. (Heather)

One of the differences between young girls and boys with Asperger's seems to be that our unusual interests are not as unusual and may seem more practical to an observer. If a girl reads voraciously, this is not as jarring or strange to a parent or physician as being fascinated with the different types of plane engines built between 1940 and 1945. But what might not be realized is that behind our bedroom door, we may be reading the same book 124 times, because we are obsessed with it. Some Aspergirls do border on trainspotting.

> I was obsessed with limestone cave formations. I never had any interest in cartoons or fantasy. (Kes)

> I liked baseball and memorized statistics with ease. (Kiley)

> I could name every car on the road before I was two. (Pokégran)

Another difference between Aspergirls and NT girls is that the latter do tend to grow out of these childhood passions and into more so-called age-appropriate activities. We will still engage in the same activities all our lives. But this isn't necessarily a bad thing. For, if Mozart wasn't obsessed with music, would not the world be the lesser for it? Temple, Einstein, even Dan Aykroyd have changed the world with their Aspergian ways. I'm sure we have had many women scientists, novelists, etc., who have contributed to culture and progress because of AS focus and diligence, but we'll never know for sure about the past. The future, however, is a different story and we may be the ones to write it. You may be one of the first *openly* autistic women to front a famous rock band, be a best-selling novelist, director, etc. Some of those women may be found right here in these pages.

ADVICE TO ASPERGIRLS

Do not let peer pressure dissuade you from doing what you love and what you are good at. Life is about making a contribution, not about being popular and fitting in.

Executive dysfunction—knowing how and when to start or stop an activity—does figure into the experience for many of us. Once we get going on something, we often do forget to eat, groom, bathe, go out, have fun; even going to work or school is an unwelcome interruption to our "zone activity." Get into the habit of taking breaks for hygiene, nutrition, and exercise. This is for your own mental and physical health—you must keep that Aspergirl machine finely tuned. This will also help increase your confidence when dealing with the outside world.

Don't worry if you don't have a savant skill—even if you spend your time in a passive activity, that may translate into a marketable skill later on. For example, an obsession for watching movies could be channeled into film school and later, a career as editor, critic, or actor. Do try to turn a passive passion into an active one. And do take at least a passing interest in other things. The more you know about life, the more informed your passion will be and the more you will feel comfortable with a variety of people and situations.

ADVICE TO PARENTS

Praise and encourage your daughter's passions, whatever they are, for therein lies her comfort, her security, her happiness, and possibly her genius. There also lies, most likely, the key to her future career.

Do not criticize her for being a bookworm, or being obsessive. She wants to please you but she can only be herself, successfully. She can try to be someone else, mirror what she thinks people want to see, but that's not who she really is. She is your gift and you are the caretaker of this special person. It is difficult at times but it is also a privilege.

On the other hand she might not have any obvious talents. A professor with AS that I interviewed said she has no savant skills, however, navigating the world of higher education for so long proves that she possesses the focus and diligence which I list as Aspie gifts. Your daughter will develop and unfold and her area of interest will appear.

2

WHY SMART GIRLS
SOMETIMES HATE SCHOOL

Despite a love of learning and an appetite for information, Aspergirls do not all enjoy school the way others might think that they would. For some, school is too slow; too restrictive, for we are often unable to read what we like or study in the areas of our passions. Social issues are yet another minefield to navigate, and an obstacle on the path to our desire—to learn as much as possible as quickly as possible.

Most of the Aspergirls said the same thing—with few exceptions, school was boring and they were bullied. *Bullying* is something that will come up throughout this book and throughout the lives of many Aspergirls. Unfortunately, it seems to be intrinsically tied to formal education. Bullying happens when someone is different and is seen as a threat in some ways, yet seen as weak in others. Aspergirls fit that bill perfectly. To a young and innocent child, bullying is a shock and often turns the world from a safe and happy place to a complete nightmare. For a spectrum child, it can be the beginning of lifelong post-traumatic stress disorder (PTSD).

I was not a classic autistic; I had no learning deficits. I was a happy, eccentric child whose Amadeus-like laughter filled the school halls and classrooms and who was tolerated if not well liked. To keep me busy, my kindergarten teacher gave me the other kids' papers to grade. It was absolute torture for me to listen to my classmates struggle with *See Jane Run*, so when my turn came, to make up for lost time, I read as fast as I possibly could—which was pretty fast. It made all the other kids giggle. Five- and six-year-olds can be much more tolerant than older kids. My uncoolness was my coolness.

Later, from about second to sixth grade, I wrote plays and gave out parts to my friends, performing them in and out of school. I had a good singing voice and wrote my own solo when the teacher gave the one Christmas solo to someone else. I had many friends...until adolescence.

All at once, my idiosyncrasies became very uncool, almost overnight. My social *deficits*, which prior to that point had just been *differences*, became glaring holes in my persona. At first I was merely ostracized, losing friends one by one, but then, the threats began. By this time I had no one to sit with at lunch so I usually spent it hiding somewhere. I developed ulcers first, by age 12. The main perpetrator of all this torment, a classic bully, announced that she was going to beat me up and that I couldn't avoid it. After a year or more of baiting me with hints of future physical pain, she finally made good her threat and I was badly beaten in front of a very large crowd of cheering kids, mostly older teenagers.

Physical fights became an almost daily probability. I went from obsessive reading to obsessive pushups to strengthen my weak limbs. Singing and laughing—my two favorite things—were supplanted by mutism and crying. I developed very low self-esteem and PTSD. And as anyone who's ever been bullied can tell you, once the air around you is poisoned, you are a target for everyone; from the strongest to the weakest, they will all want to take a shot at you.

How does a girl who was once a gifted and *popular* student fall so far? Home was dysfunctional, and I'd already become mute and withdrawn there, long before I did at school. My teachers may have noticed, but as is often the case, the bully was more popular with teachers than I was. Kim wasn't a know-it-all like I was; she didn't appear sullen and awkward, but instead, was confident and gregarious. It is possible, if not likely, that some teachers thought I had it coming.

Teachers, more often than not, either can't or won't protect you. While a good teacher is an incredible gift to a child's life and mind, a bad one is a force for destruction.

> The bullying started in my first year of kindergarten which was in 1985. We were all sitting in our chairs at our assigned tables and working on an art project when I felt this extreme need to stand up and spin around and around in circles and stare up at the ceiling. The teacher grabbed me by my hair and dragged me into the coatroom where she began to beat me with a ruler. She told me I had been disruptive to the class. The students could see through the little window of the coatroom door and thought it was funny. After this incident the children started to torment me on a daily basis. It started off with name calling, but then quickly progressed to kicking, punching, pulling of hair, biting me; things of that nature. After being held back twice, I was given tests. I was then enrolled into a gifted and talented program during the summer months, held at a different school in a different district. It was only during these months of school that I ever felt that I fit in with other students. (Brandi)

Having AS means you have both talents and deficits—recognition of both is important, but even when a girl is diagnosed it doesn't necessarily mean she will thrive. I don't think individualized education plans (IEPs) existed when I was in school, but from what Aspergirls tell me, they don't always do what they are set out to do.

> I had a gifted IEP. Middle school and high school were hell—bullying from students and teachers, no one to turn to. I spent years dealing with severe depression. Everyone ignored my problems because I had good grades. (Andi)

Again and again throughout the conversations with Aspergirls I heard stories that echoed my own. For some the bullying started earlier or later, but it almost always starts. While bullying happens to both males and females on the spectrum, girls, particularly, can be judgmental. Dr. Grandin advocates that some gifted children with autism should be allowed to skip high school and go right to college and I couldn't agree with her more. We flourish much better in an environment where the emphasis is on academic achievement and not socializing. Of course we need to learn to socialize, but through shared interests with like-minded individuals, not by being thrown to the lions. Emotionally, we *require* an atmosphere of tolerance and non-judgment.

> With NT girls, you just don't know what the game is about. They have a coldness that can turn to meanness. (Widders)

With diagnosis or an IEP we might end up in special ed or some other place where some well-meaning individuals watch us like hawks, which we do not like. Barring learning deficits like dyslexia it is our emotions that really need the extra care. Our intellect will do just fine if you give it something to play with and let it go. (Reminder: I am referring to high-functioning individuals.)

Even if you are not bullied at school, it can still be very lonely. The reason many adults with AS like to be alone is because we simply get used to it, starting at an early age. I know we all have a fight-or-flight reaction to others, but I think that is an acquired response, even if it is acquired very early on.

I get let out of class early to avoid the crowds and I don't have to eat in the lunch room. I hope I find a friend. Someone who understands me. (Megan)

Experiences in school (grade school particularly) differ from one Aspergirl to the next and certainly from one school to the next. The soul of a school is comprised of its people. We are all individuals and there is no blanket remedy for any of these situations. Some Aspergirls thrived in the days before diagnosis, scrutiny, IEPs and special ed, partly because they *were* left alone, and partly because bullies were not allowed to conduct their reign of terror.

In Catholic primary schools in those days it was Aspie Paradise. Schooling was strict, formal and predictable. I thrived. It was expected that children would work hard, obey rules and be kind to one another. (Pokégran)

Aspergirls do not thrive under scrutiny, if it has just the slightest bit of hostility in it. Whether from our peers or teachers, if we are looked at with an unfriendly, intimidating, or threatening eye, we fold. Alone, we are talented, graceful, witty, and smart, but under such circumstances we curl up like hedgehogs. We're as sensitive emotionally as we are physically and the bullying becomes a vicious cycle—when the perpetrators see what an effect they're having, they redouble their efforts. Some of us get backed into a corner and keep retreating until we are out in the parking lot…then we just keep going. In other words, we quit. Some of us older Aspergirls went from gifted student to high school or college dropout. Instead of getting PhDs, we let PTSD stop us at our GED (General Equivalency Diploma or General Education Diploma). Quitting is better than allowing someone to bully us to death. We feel powerful when we leave a bad situation, for it means we are taking control, something very important to an Aspergian. But the problem comes in the future, when we realize we are 42 and never got that degree, or didn't get as high a degree as we should have. Our temporary feeling of triumph will come back to bite us in the backside again and again.

We, or at least our parents, have the power of choice. If you are not doing well, another school might provide a dramatically different experience.

> Public school was a struggle. I was bullied, teased; I was shy and slow. I had difficulty reading due to dyslexia. High school was a private international school, and I was encouraged to grow as an individual. I did well there. (Jen)

ADVICE TO ASPERGIRLS

Socializing is a big part of the school experience, just ask anyone who has ever had to sit alone at lunch every day. Try to find friends who will accept you as you are, rather than trying to hang with the cool kids. But do make the most of the learning opportunities. While you may want to run straight home after school, joining extracurricular activities might put you in touch with people with similar interests; you may find another Aspergirl in the drama or science club. There are many more of us around than previously thought. Do not suffer in silence and risk eating and psychological disorders—keep searching till you find a friend who understands AS and your issues.

I hear from people on the spectrum all the time who are being bullied at home, at school, and at work. They are often afraid to speak up or to make waves for fear it will get worse. There is nothing worse than being bullied. Being bullied will result in shattered nerves and poorer mental and physical health. Aspergirls, you need advocacy and protection, but you also need to stand up for yourself. That includes *seeking* help and advocacy, not necessarily confronting the bullies directly. There are a number of resources out there which provide strategies for dealing with bullying and gossip, including my employment book *Asperger's on the Job* (Simone 2010). There are also websites with steps to follow. Get help. Tell your parents you won't go back to that school until the bullying stops. My own daughter was being ridiculed at a school she went to, so I home-schooled her and then took her across town to a better one once I found it. She's not autistic, but the point is, every parent should have a zero tolerance for bullying when it comes to their child.

Look yourself, or ask your parents to look for a school for Aspies. My dream school would be an all-Aspergirl school and although I do not know of one at this time, I think it is inevitable that one will soon exist.

Some of the Aspergirls I interviewed were bullied and abused by parents. If your parent bullies you, find another relative to protect you. If you have difficulty describing what is going on, write it down and give it to someone who is in a position to assist you, someone you trust. Abuse is not something you should have to tolerate. Protect yourself, feel no guilt, and get help!

ADVICE TO PARENTS

Your child is smart—*you* know that and *they* know that, but teachers, peers, administration, and counselors might not see it. Many people equate Asperger syndrome with intellectual impairment and that is one of the risks of disclosure. On the other hand, she may be obviously smart and it isn't any fun to hear other kids struggling with *See Jane Run* while you're already on Dickens. If your child is gifted, she might need a special program or some challenge in her life. Remember however, that she may seem quite mature in many ways but she is autistic and she will be fragile and childlike in others. Letting her be moved up a grade or two might not be a good idea if she feels intimidated by older kids. Happiness achieved through being allowed to be herself is more important than academic achievement, for it is the foundation on which the latter will be built.

There are schools specifically for kids with AS. Keep checking as this is a topic that is exploding and I'm sure it is only a matter of time before there are some all-girl Aspie schools.

Regarding bullying

Parents—you *must* protect your children even if part of that protection means teaching and encouraging them to stand up for themselves. But there are times that bullying is health- and life-threatening and intervention is needed. Don't be afraid to make waves when there's so much at stake. Just because a school says it has a zero tolerance policy for bullying doesn't mean it's true. Don't be afraid to switch your daughter's school. She may balk at the idea even if she hates her current school because she doesn't like change, but if she's in danger of either academic underachievement, social isolation or bullying, you might want to seriously consider this option.

3

SENSORY OVERLOAD

There are a million triggers lurking everywhere, waiting to set us off, steal our peace and sabotage our calm. Sights, sounds, smells, touches, and even tastes can drain us mentally, physically, and emotionally. Why do things that others barely notice send us into a tailspin—literally? I personally subscribe to the "Intense World" theory of autism (Markram, Rinaldi and Markram 2007). Markram states that we are hyp*er*functional as opposed to hyp*o*functional. People used to think that autistics felt less, felt nothing, were less than human in some ways. Actually the opposite is true—we feel everything, we smell everything, we hear everything...and we sense things others can't. There is no heterogeneity in autism, so some people might not experience this; a couple of the Aspergirls said they felt very little as children. But most will agree that we feel things "too much." I'm reminded of Lucy's character in *Dracula*: "I hear mice in the attic stomping around like elephants." We fixate on little tiny things that other people barely notice. Not because we are neurotic, not because we are attention-grabbers, but because those things are jumping out at us.

The Aspergirls I interviewed gave me quite a long, long list of what sets them off. Here's just a small part of it:

Loud social situations, traffic, standing in queues, perfume, fluorescent lights, clothing labels, background noise on phone, music in shops, when someone is fiddling, cigarettes, air fresheners, babies crying, vacuums, bathroom ceiling fans, sirens, fire alarms, fireworks, yelling/arguing, car horns, power tools, loud music in cars, TVs everywhere, commercials, cell phone ring-tones, if two people talk to me at once, too many items on shelves, cities, wind, cold…

The list was much *much* longer, but you get the general idea. But knowing what triggers we have is not the same as knowing what it feels like, or why. I think that most people who are not on the spectrum think of a sensory *trigger* as more like a phobia. A windy day makes you anxious not because of an irrational fear, but because trees are swaying, their leaves swirling, branches waving chaotically. The sound of wind is loud, distracting, an unpredictable assault on the ears. The wind pulls your hair and whips it into your face and eyes; it tugs on clothes and aggravates the skin—this is sensory overload.

Sensory processing disorder is a separate syndrome, but it's part of autism's package deal. Most if not all of us will have it to some degree.

SOUNDS

A cuckoo clock goes off unexpectedly. Two people carry on talking while a third doubles over and puts her hands over her ears—why? It is not, for most of us, a problem with the ears but a processing difference. Despite our legendary ability to focus, or perhaps because of it, we tend to need to address one noise at a time, so if we are on the phone, the television must be muted. If we are in conversation, the radio must be off. If someone is fidgeting while I'm trying to speak on the phone, they have to leave the room or they have to stop. Even the most minor movement and sound is a distraction.

> Typical sounds that others can filter out, drive me to *distraction*...and shatter into shards of disorienting pain. (Stella)

Our sensitivity to sound as well as touch strongly affects our sleep habits and many of us can't catch 40 winks without earplugs and noiseless, heavy blankets. Because we have minds like recorders, even hearing a song before bed means it might play over and over again, robbing us of our rest. We have to limit what we take in and we must be selective.

A lot of these triggers, perhaps all of them, exist only in relation to our lack of control over them. If I'm running the lawnmower and making a racket, that is okay, but if my neighbor is, that's a different story. This can make us seem like control freaks to others, and a bit hypocritical to boot. After all, some of us play in rock bands, or love heavy metal. But that means that we are *prepared* for it. We can handle an onslaught of sound for a time, but preferably a time, place and sound of our choosing. Hence, therapy for sound sensitivities may involve playing recordings of sounds that upset you and controlling the interval and volume until you get used to it and it no longer bothers you.

SIGHTS

We all know that Autistics and Aspies have an aversion to fluorescent lights because they flicker and hum at a rate we can detect even when others can't. But there are many other visual processing difficulties, such as from too many objects or people in motion. The objects in a grocery store aren't in motion but we are, causing a maelstrom of images in our minds that make us dizzy like we're riding the scrambler at the county fair. Grocery stores are hell on earth for autistic children and grownup Aspergirls don't like large shops any better—and yes, they can still cause us to have temper tantrums. We'll take a small boutique over a department store any day.

Recently I spent a day walking and exploring the historic city of Boston. By the end of it, even though I'd worn ear plugs and shades and had paced myself, I had taken in too many things for my brain to process. I had unnecessary images and sounds in my head that needed releasing. As I tried to sleep, these pictures played in my mind like a kaleidoscope, each one appearing and then morphing into the next. It was so vivid and full-color that it was like looking at a movie screen. While it was happening, my temperature shot up to a fever. My body was frantically working to "rid" itself of this invasion as if it were a virus. This went on for an hour or two before it slowed and I was able to sleep. Sometimes we just can't get rid of unwanted images so we may be quite selective about what we want to see. Other people might see us as being fussy, difficult to please, oversensitive, and they may hesitate to invite us out anywhere for fear we won't like it. They just don't understand the intensity and repercussions of so-called normal stimuli.

> I can't watch a lot of movies because of the imagery. I don't like having the images stuck in my head for eternity. I made the mistake of watching *Hostel* once, and to this day I could draw the worst scenes in it direct from memory. (Andi)

SKIN SENSITIVITY

The Aspergian need for soft fabrics and a firm touch is well known. We all have aversions to certain products and fabrics, though what those are vary from one individual to the next. Uncomfortable, fussy clothing is a torture for most people with Asperger's, not just females, but females have more fashion choices and may be expected on some level to wear fussy things.

If you don't believe me just go to any shop: ruffles, strings, lace, polyester, wires, straps. We don't like fussy and we don't like frilly. Some of us like soft, tight undergarments like camisoles and leggings, to keep cold air off our skin. Others may only wear loose-fitting things. Always soft.

Little autistic kids are supersensitive to clothing and may not be able to tell you. It has always been fashionable for little girls to be dressed in "baby doll" outfits, with puffy sleeves that have elastic bands at the arms and thighs. Those clothes are torture; by the end of the day those elastic bands cut into flesh. Crocheted baby blankets do nothing to keep us warm at night but we can't tell our mothers because we are still non-verbal, so we freeze. When we're older, our mothers don't dress us but we are "dressed" by societal expectations, the uniforms of our positions, and by available fashions and fabrics. Currently it's much better for Aspergirls than it was decades ago, say in the 1950s and 1960s. At least we aren't expected to have a stiff bouffant and wear heaps of nylon and wool, but we still have a lot of fashion hurdles to deal with, for example, pantyhose and high heels, swishy dresses, scratchy shirts, binding bras, and pinching trousers. We usually hate the cold, so we wrap ourselves in layers of soft, warm, frumpy clothing rather than something more becoming. Aspergirls are notorious for dressing for comfort before style. This can give others the perception that we don't care about our appearance, that we're unfeminine, a bit lower-class. While we want to be found attractive, we can't see ourselves as others do and we can't sacrifice comfort for acceptance. When we find something that fits, is comfortable, *and* is fashionable, it's like finding the Holy Grail.

We only like tight hugs, but those aren't appropriate in all situations so we'll avoid polite hugs people seem to enjoy giving each other. I always wonder how European Aspies deal with all those kisses on the cheek. They make me rub my face like a five-year-old boy after Aunt Mildred slobbers on him. This is also easy to misperceive as being cold and unaffectionate. We are affectionate when we want to be and particularly when we can control the amount of physical pressure involved.

PSYCHIC SENSITIVITY

That is not a misprint. I believe that in some cases, our senses are heightened and are almost animal-like. We sense things. Many people think that those with AS are psychically blind but I do not agree. Again this may be more germane to females, as psychic sensitivity (woman's intuition) is somewhat split along gender lines anyway. I think, similar to our sense of humor, we miss the obvious and see what is not obvious to others.

> I have what some call psychic experiences and always have. To me, it seems perfectly logical. After all, there is the need to communicate and when your brain doesn't want you to communicate "normally," it seems to compensate in this way. (Dame Kev)

I can tell you that I dreamt of 9/11 hours before it happened and also had a vision of the 2004 tsunami when I was in Thailand, ten months before it occurred. I'm sure you won't believe that, but you might agree that cats and other animals can sense earthquakes, even though that too is not proven by science. Just because science can't prove it—yet—doesn't mean it doesn't exist.

I believe that this is a large part of why we have difficulty getting along with others. If someone is smiling and saying one thing but psychically we are hearing something completely different, we will get confused and want to run away. This often conflicts with appearances and what others tell me, causing me to doubt my own intuition. I usually turn out to be right. A more cynical person might call it a self-fulfilling prophecy. The misperception of this sensitivity is that we are hard to get along with...paranoid.

Sensory problems affect us everywhere. They make dating difficult: "Is this new guy gonna think I'm a freak if a siren goes off and I have to cover my ears and flee?"; they affect employment: "Do I really want to spend $300 a year on itchy nylons?"; and everything else as well: "I'd like to go out but it's too noisy/cold/windy…"

The fallout? *We stay home a lot.*

ADVICE TO ASPERGIRLS

Stress and sensory overload need to be looked at as a total package. Environmental sensitivity will always exist for most of us with AS but our reactions to triggers can be managed through taking good care of ourselves in general. You must take good care of your body and your nerves so when that cart rolls by with the squeaky wheel, or the fire alarm goes off, you may jump but you won't fall to pieces. What can we do?

Exercise

Many of us are more in our minds than in our bodies, and we think just because we focus on work or hobbies 14 hours a day and are tired, that we have exercised. We haven't. Try things that integrate the mind, body, and spirit—yoga does that and might appeal more to an Aspergirl than an aerobics class, with its oft-obnoxious music. Yoga works on releasing chi and channeling it into parts of the body where it is blocked—including the brain. When I was teaching yoga I was much more mentally and physically calm. Martial arts or dance might work; pilates, or a mini-trampoline—it's repetitive and you don't have to join a gym, just buy one. Exercise bikes and ellipticals are also tools you can keep at home. Aspergirls are not gym-goers. We don't like the atmosphere, and there's too many strangers for us to feel comfortable, especially with all the emphasis on the body, but we can still work out. Try jogging, skating, or jumping rope.

Diet

Diet is important—stay away from chemicals, sugars, and any processed food. There are more stringent autism-specific diets as well, including the gluten-free, casein-free (GFCF) and the specific carbohydrate (SCD) diets. We'll talk more about that in Chapter 19.

Therapies

These are being developed all the time for people on the spectrum, not just for social skills but also sensory issues; usually some form of cognitive behavioral therapy (CBT).

Equipment

Sunglasses or colored lenses, hats, earplugs, iPods, comfortable clothing, and a squishy toy in your pocket can prevent overload before it happens. Take water and anything else you need to keep yourself hydrated and nourished when out and about.

Make informed choices

Make informed choices about what you're going to do and where you're going to do it. I've moved a lot but always live near an open field, park, lake, or ocean. This is because, even before AS awareness, I knew that I needed to have visual quiet as well as auditory stillness. For the last few years, particularly, I have avoided cities and places that I know will flood me with sights and sounds that I am unable to process in "real time." You might like the *idea* of living in New York City but you might not be able to handle the constant sensory overload of it.

Some people create *sensory rooms* to regulate themselves if they feel a meltdown coming on or to recover from one afterward. Sensory rooms have special lights, smells, sounds, temperatures, and textures which you choose yourself to provide deep soothing input to your individual senses.

ADVICE TO PARENTS

If there are distinct triggers that you know of then try to avoid them. There are literally countless triggers everywhere we go. Watch for signs of physical and emotional discomfort in your child and don't expect them to just "get over it." Remove the source or remove them from the source. Sensory triggers are real and strong aversions, not just petty annoyances. They can leave us feeling sick and depleted. Work on getting the various therapies that help us minimize our reactions to triggers.

If you have a young Aspergirl and need to take her shopping, let her get used to stores a little at a time, one or two aisles at most. Let her identify markers along the way—where her favorite foods are, so she'll be able to fathom it better the next time she comes in. Hats and sunglasses will help, earplugs and iPods for older girls. Though they may make it hard to communicate with her the benefits will outweigh that inconvenience.

4

STIMMING, AND WHAT WE DO WHEN WE'RE HAPPY

What happens when we experience sensory or emotional overload? Well, different things. Sometimes we get migraines, nausea, sometimes we have meltdowns, and sometimes we just *stim*.

I hate the word stimming. First of all I think it sounds creepy and weird, second of all it's a misnomer. Stimming is short for self-stimulatory behavior, but that's not exactly what it is. Stimming is simply something we do to *soothe* ourselves when we are upset, anxious, overloaded, or in pain; to release unpleasant feelings or energy. A student of eastern thought might say we have blocked *chi—life force*; energy.

Stimming behaviors typically include rocking, swaying, twirling, spinning (yourself or objects), humming, flapping, tapping, clapping, finger flicking, and so on. I'm sure there are many, many more. Soothing stims happen because someone or something is pushing our autistic buttons.

Little kids stim when they're bored, which makes them anxious; they stim when they've had sugary things with artificial coloring because it makes their bodies feel twitchy. They stim because the supermarket has too many items in it and the lights hurt their eyes. They stim when grownups are yelling and they stim when other kids are mean. They stim from the million and one triggers that are all around.

As adults, we stim when the rent is due and we're short, or we need new tires, or we have to get up early and go some place and don't know exactly where it is or what to expect. We stim because we have to go to dinner with…(gasp!) people. We stim when we're lonely and sad. We stim thinking about any stressful activity we might have to engage in.

The earliest stims I remember doing were spinning tops and rocking on my horse—all socially acceptable for little girls. Like Donna Williams, I also remember watching the patterns in the air but in my case, in the darkness when I closed my eyes. Red and white circles swam against the blackness, and it was infinitely entertaining and soothing. When I needed to change it up, I pressed my eyeballs or squeezed the sides together to make a whole new burst of swimming circles. That is one stim I don't do anymore. Now, all grown up, I hum tunelessly; after giving a lecture, I have to run through the parking lot to my car. I don't care who sees me. If I'm very stressed, I'll put my hands on either side of my head and squeeze and rock. It's better than having a meltdown or getting an ulcer.

We stim from sensory issues, and we stim from anxiety and social or emotional issues. When you read this list of stims, I want you to keep in mind that the women speaking are of all ages, and some are highly successful and/or educated:

Bounce on a ball or trampoline, play with toys, flap my arms, rub certain fabrics, bite my nails, rock (side to side or back and forth), spin things; kick my feet in patterns, drum rhythms on surfaces, face-rub with the back of my left wrist, wriggle constantly, tap thumb and forefingers together, pace, sway, and shift from leg to leg, whisper things I've memorized, finger flick, wiggle my fingers, or rub them together. Rock on heels while in public, hum monotonically, sing, repeat things, talk to myself, rub my belly; pet my dog, stare at clouds, watch favorite movies repeatedly, match my breaths with each syllable in a sentence.

Autistic people have an innocence, a childlike quality, regardless of age or education. This is very obvious when we are anxious and upset.

> I'm a very tactile person (to materials and objects, not other people!), so I tend to soothe myself by touching either a material that I like—book-bindings in leather for example; or an object that I like—an action figure out of my personal collection, or some of my son's stuffed animals. (Siv)

By the time we grow up, we know what isn't acceptable to do in public but sometimes we forget ourselves.

> In public, if I am getting overwhelmed I will jiggle my leg or tap my fingers—small stims which are probably somewhat annoying to others, but don't mark me as a complete loony. (Polly)

> I don't consciously realize I'm doing it. In public, I try to sit still if I'm worried what people think of me. I've embarrassed myself a few times, especially in restaurants where people tend to stare. (Andi)

But there is a trade-off to self-control. Not stimming when you feel anxious means you're not releasing the build-up of tension and you risk having a meltdown, or migraine, or acquiring a *tic*. Sometimes my eyes or mouth will twitch and that is totally involuntary. Some tics are semi-involuntary. I had a vocal tic when I was little—I made a clicking noise in my throat. Perhaps that is a perseveration. *Perseverations* are gestures, movements, or repetitive rituals we cannot stop ourselves from doing and so straddle that line between tic, stim, and ritual. I didn't know anyone could hear my clicking, so I didn't try to contain it. I suppose it was in lieu of rocking or something more noticeable, but the trouble was, it *was* noticeable and I didn't know it until my best friend said "What is that stupid noise you always make in your throat?" I was horrified and found the will power to stop. I'm sure it was probably replaced by nail-biting or something else that was fairly socially acceptable. The trouble with repressing stims is that we tend to pick up destructive habits, or else we just internalize our anxieties and pains instead of releasing them as they happen.

> My mom saw me rocking one day in the kitchen when I was young and said "What's wrong with you? You retarded?" After that I started bouncing my feet off the foot board, driving my little sister in the bottom bunk crazy. In public I'm a mess. I pick at invisible hairs, clean dirt out from under my nails over and over, and fidget with everything I'm wearing. Picked up smoking at 20, having a hard time beating that one. (Bramble)

Our emotions are raw, immature, childlike. Nowhere is this more apparent than when we get excited. I asked the Aspergirls if they "stim" when they're excited and I got the following list—they are very similar to our anxiety stims; but they happen because of an overflow of positive emotion:

> Dance for joy, laugh out loud, flap my hands or arms, say "yay" and "yippee" like a little kid, jump up and down, ball up my fists and shake them, clap, can't stop laughing, pace back and forth at full speed, skip, sing, speak in a high squeaky voice.

> A lot of my obsessions tend to be media based (certain TV shows/movies, for instance) so if I'm at a particularly good bit, I might have to pause it, have a quick run, and then continue. (Polly)

Many of the Aspergirls mentioned a high-pitched laugh or squeak when happy, and a childish tone of voice. I do think this display of exuberance is more germane to girls and is relatively socially acceptable for us and so we are lucky in some respects. How socially acceptable depends on the situation and the mindset of the people we're with.

> When everyone's in a goofy mood, nobody seems to point out my quirks so much. (Dame Kev)

> People don't seem to mind, and some seem to enjoy things more because I get really excited about them. (Andi)

Some parents put their Aspergirls in dance or other classes to channel that energy into something more constructive or socially acceptable.

> My mother insisted I use all of that energy for something productive. The solution was dance, martial arts, tennis, fencing, or any type of sport that forced me to learn to channel that exuberance. It also helps keep me from jumping on someone unexpectedly for a wrastle. (Dame Kev)

Others haven't found acceptable outlets so they've learned to suppress or channel "happiness stims" into something less noticeable, often after being made fun of or criticized.

> I noticed I was different as a teen when someone said "What's wrong with you?" I was jumping up and down at the time. At some point I got into the habit of keeping my hands clasped and held in front of my waist when walking. When I'm happy, that morphs into thumb twiddling. I'm not sure when I got into those habits. They're less noticeable though, I think. (Elfinia)

> The more I learn about Asperger's, the more I realize how much of who I am (and was) was constantly being covered: "Don't do that, don't look that way, be polite,"

etc. I am hopeful for myself now and for my kids to understand themselves and to love those differences. I am also bringing back some of the old stims which were taken away from me—jumping on the tramp, spinning tops, clapping. (Jen)

Stims are harmless, usually—recently, a favorite song came on the iPod (I didn't know my daughter had put it on for me) and I flapped my hands in excitement, which is fine except I was driving on the thruway. It caused me to lose control of the car for just a moment—I had not been aware of that tendency prior to that incident.

It makes it difficult to go out and have fun when we know that if we are just ourselves, people will think we're strange. Fear of ridicule is just one more thing that keeps us isolated. Others' misperceptions might be that we're immature, mentally challenged, or that we're acting silly on purpose to attract attention. Since we are often stoic, when we're happy and exuberant, it can be misconstrued as flirting.

ADVICE TO ASPERGIRLS

We do develop some control over when, how and where we "release chi." How much you want to stim in public is up to you. I realize that perhaps there are some things better left in private. But if I'm not hurting anyone or causing a loved one terrible embarrassment, I will let it all hang out. I jump up and down, flap, clap, skip, talk in a high squeaky voice, and laugh gleefully. Since I've allowed myself this freedom of expression, I feel healthier, I feel happier. I love all of these things about myself. My facial tics have almost completely gone away except in times of extreme stress.

I tell people that I may rock or flap or whatever to alert and educate them about what autism/Asperger's really is. Recently I flew on a plane and there was turbulence. I explained to the person next to me that I needed to rock because I was scared. After the bumpy ride was over, I asked if it was weird for her to see. "No," she replied, "I almost wanted to join you."

I don't want to spend a lot of time in environments or around people that can't handle the real me. But I do realize some of you are in jobs or communities that are a bit straight-laced. Let your hair down when you can. Make sure that at least some of the time, you can let it all out, or from what other Aspergirls tell me and from my own experience, you will damage yourself— your nerves, your psyche, and you will diminish your potential for happiness. Smile and stim. Stim and smile. Sure is better for you than smoking.

ADVICE TO PARENTS

You don't want your daughter to draw attention to herself for being strange, and you don't want the other kids to make fun of her so you might find yourself being a bit strict and critical of these types of demonstrations.

If your child is engaged in an anxiety stim then try to figure out what is bothering her and fix or eliminate it. Maybe she has sensory overload. Maybe she needs some intelligent conversation or engaging interaction. Maybe she needs to be given a challenge or a chore. If you're around others maybe there is someone who is giving her an unpleasant feeling.

Yelling at her for acting this way is just going to make her feel ashamed, and if it's a happiness stim she's doing it'll ruin the joy of the moment. Help her to channel it into something useful, constructive and socially acceptable. If you daughter likes to jump up and down, buy her a trampoline; if she likes to twirl, get her dance lessons; if she likes to hum, encourage voice lessons or joining a choir. Tapping can be channeled into drumming and so on.

Being embarrassed about whether or not your Aspergirl is going to stim in public is no different than worrying about what your fellow church-goers will think about her pierced nose. It's about your vanity to some degree; your reputation. But she is who she is. God (if you believe in God) gave her to you to nurture and to protect and also to let flourish.

If her stims are self-injuring, that is something else entirely. Most of the Aspergirls I spoke to only self-injured when on the wrong medication, when benign stimming was discouraged, or when there was some serious psychodrama going on in their young life, such as abuse or bullying. Find out the source. Don't be too quick to medicate without thorough research, whether it's garden-variety stimming or self-injury. We'll talk more about medication later.

5

ON BLAME AND
INTERNALIZING GUILT

Lists of Asperger traits say that we have difficulty with eye contact, which makes us look guilty to the uninitiated. I think there's more to it than that. I think we internalize a lot of guilt along the way.

In addition to the embarrassment of having our stims pointed out to us, we will have all of our other idiosyncrasies pointed out as well, one after another, starting when we're young—by our families, our friends, our teachers, and everyone else who might be a witness. We are blamed for our erratic and often uncontrollable behavior. Even those who were well behaved were blamed for social awkwardness and botched interactions. Because we never knew what we did wrong, a profound sense of confusion, alienation, and *guilt* crept into our psyches, displacing normal childhood emotions.

> I displayed many autistic behaviors. It was assumed I *knew* I was acting weird, and did it deliberately. I. Just. Did. Not. Get. It! (Polly)

> During my early home life I was not diagnosed and my symptoms were overlooked. I was told to "buck up" or

"stop it" if I was having problems with school and social interaction. (Brandi)

If there is no diagnosis then there is a vacuum—a hole in which to pour speculation and fill with labels.

> School counselors thought I was a brat. I went to many psychiatrists and took many tests and was diagnosed at 12. (Riley)

Diagnosis still doesn't always stop the people around the Aspergirl from thinking that she is somehow reacting to things "on purpose." Families and communities, out of ignorance or sometimes jealousy, will often accuse her of faking reactions, drawing attention to herself, or even choosing to have meltdowns. Parents who are supportive may end up sharing blame and receiving criticism themselves from other family members who may not take the time to read about and understand AS.

> My daughter was diagnosed very young. Ever since I can remember, my family thought we were too indulgent and that she needed stricter discipline. They could not understand how we could "allow" her temper tantrums, and how we could allow her to not socialize with others. As she grew, the family changed the way they treated her. They went from feeling she was a spoiled child to treating her almost as if she were retarded. When her cousins get together to socialize, they never include her. My mother was afraid of her, and was uncomfortable being alone with her. (Deborah)

It's bad enough if a little boy acts like a wild thing in public but "girls should know better" how to behave.

> I would meltdown and my parents would threaten to commit me if I didn't quit. (Naga Empress)

Blamed for lots of social interactions going wrong. Never understood what I did most of the time. They would just say "You know what you did!" I never did. (Elfinia)

The potential fallout to this, on top of having AS, is having a life-long guilt complex; becoming apathetic to even trying to have friendships or relationships; and being fairly easy to goad into things. We often, as children and as adults, try extra hard to please and not to make waves, but somehow we always end up "causing problems." We may try very hard to behave. We think that if we are very, very good, people will like us and all will be well. I see this all the time with adults with AS at their jobs. They try not to make waves, but still they get accused of things and they don't understand it.

When puberty hits things get worse instead of better. We might start engaging in the very behavior of which we are accused. If everyone says you're a troublemaker, you've nothing to lose by actually making trouble.

I lived in a very controlling, hostile environment. Everything I did was watched under close eye with immediate criticism. Nothing I did was right. I was not allowed to do much. I displayed social avoidance, selective mutism, horrible eye contact, soft, slurred speech, rocking, constant fidgeting. Being that I am a female this was all considered shyness, then they chalked it up to puberty, then it was being a young adult. I was always told, "You'll grow out of it." (Elle)

But of course we never do grow out of it. One of the things that has recurred throughout my life is a feeling that I *should* be doing better, that I should be able to handle a job/relationship/ life/whatever, better than I am. Every time someone walked out of my life—whether friend, boyfriend, husband, boss, etc. they always said "You're strong, you'll be just fine." But I did not feel strong. I felt incredibly flawed and vulnerable and just couldn't figure out why. I knew my mind was strong, and I knew I wasn't insane, or at least I hoped. I had doctors and counselors list my various behavioral problems, most of which, in hindsight, fall onto the list for AS: fear of change, emotional immaturity, obsessive behavior, need for control, inflexibility, depression, self-absorption. But rather than symptoms they sounded more like judgments, as if knowing what the problem was I should therefore, be able to change it—*because I'm obviously intelligent.* Needless to say, I didn't stay with those counselors very long. I came to the conclusion that there was nothing wrong with me, there was something wrong with everyone else. That worked for a while, until I had a daughter, and she also had the same observations, with a few more of her own thrown in, for example weird; socially awkward. I felt utterly alone. Then I discovered Asperger's.

Once we receive the diagnosis, whether through the efforts of a perceptive doctor or our own investigative work, there is definitely relief; a laying down of our burden. But that burden gets picked up again and again, every time someone asks "Why can't you just?" or every time we simply just *can't.* New situations will constantly arise that push our sensory buttons, cause us to panic, trigger meltdowns, etc. Knowing you have AS is not going to fix all these things, nor is it going to make you suddenly socially adept. And not everyone you meet is going to realize you are on the spectrum, so they are going to be measuring your behavior with a non-autistic yardstick.

There is always going to be some internalization of blame. Most of us, whether we care to admit it or not, have a considerable amount of embarrassment and shame to contend with—for not being able to handle the little day-to-day, ordinary experiences that other women seem to manage just fine. Whether that means holding down a job or a conversation; growing friendships or savings accounts, as a group it is safe to say that we struggle with these things.

We feel guilt for another reason—Asperger's is not an obvious, life-threatening condition like cancer or some other horrible disease or situation, and we know it. We look "normal"; we are often extremely smart. Some of us may not have any learning deficits at all, others do but they're usually not obvious, for example dyslexia. When others tell us to "deal with it" we wish that we could, and part of us thinks that we *should*. But telling a person with Asperger's to just "get on with it" is like telling a person in a wheelchair to take the stairs if they want to get to the second floor.

Men have their own pressures but women, who are expected by society to be capable, multi-tasking, high heel wearing, doyennes of manners, etiquette and the sharp retort, will feel it in their own special way.

ADVICE TO ASPERGIRLS

Some family members will read all they can about Asperger's and get behind you 100 percent. Some won't lift a finger to try and understand. They may think they've got you all figured out and they won't want to hear anything that challenges their assumptions and makes them examine their own behavior towards you. Most will fall somewhere in the middle. If you're older and your parents are elderly they may not be mentally prepared at this stage to believe that you're autistic and that they never noticed it.

If you had a rough start in life, and were unsupported, I was going to tell you not to let it cloud your mind, prejudice it against people, because there are good people out there in the world, and you will find them. But the truth is, every person you meet in your life will have good and bad traits, positive and negative qualities. Some will have more good than others. Some will see things in you that they admire, that they resonate with, and others will see your so-called weaknesses as an invitation to criticize, bully, etc. Some will want to befriend you, nurture you, and even protect you, while others will exploit and abuse. Some people may do both things at varying times. I have lived for many years with this condition and my own family still doesn't get me. Although they know I have something to do with AS awareness and education, they will praise me in one breath, question my Aspergian behavior in the next.

The best thing you can do is believe in yourself and know that there is good in most people. You can bring it out in them if you know how to. A tuning fork, when you strike it, can make a guitar string resonate with the same note if it's close enough in pitch. You are special, you have special qualities, and you can bring out similar qualities in other people. You can spur them to examine life from a perspective that they contain within themselves, but rarely bring out into the light. You are here for a purpose and a reason. You grace the world with your presence, and there *will* be people who appreciate you. As you get older I hope that your confidence increases rather than decreases and that you don't shut yourself away in your bedroom as so many of us do, watching films or reading books every night because we know what the world consists of and we don't like it. If you don't like your immediate environment—town, city, etc. perhaps you need to get creative and decide where you can put yourself to do the most good (once you're old enough). Don't let the rat race get you so down that you end up in the "rut race"—an even worse game where you are just spinning wheels and spending time.

Hopefully your family are supportive. If they aren't, I know how difficult and lonely it is to exist in a household where you are made to feel the black sheep. It's funny, but a dysfunctional family, if they don't know they're dysfunctional, can make *you* feel like the dysfunctional one because you don't fit in. I firmly believe that most of the psychological problems that seem to come with AS have more to do with non-acceptance, bullying, and blaming than anything else. Someday you will be able to leave and have your own family and you can set the tone for your house—one filled with light, love, games, creativity, reading, humor, and whatever else you want...even if it's 15 ferrets and a llama.

ADVICE TO PARENTS

First of all, don't blame yourself or your husband because your daughter is an Aspergirl. Second, don't blame her. You have a gift and a blessing on your hands.

> It's funny, I think all moms who genuinely love and care for their children think that anything that's not perfect with their child is somehow the mom's "fault." I had a terrible virus in the first trimester of my pregnancy. I beat myself up over this for months. What if I hadn't worked in the doctor's office...maybe I wouldn't have gotten sick...or maybe I shouldn't have worked but just stayed home and taken care of myself... You can make yourself crazy with guilt sometimes. But I came to realize life is what it is. With age comes wisdom. I had no real control over my daughter's outcomes. And shame on me for ever thinking that she is less of a person for her "disability." With or without Asperger's, I couldn't love her more, and she is the perfect being God intended her to be. Shame on doctors and therapists who put blame on others for their children's not fitting into the mold of normalcy. People with labels are no more or less. They count as much as we do, and bring so much color into what could be a very boring black and white existence. I think it is important that parents of children (young or adult) understand that. (Deborah Tedone, director of Square Pegs/Asperger's Support Group)

Your Aspergirl may be difficult at times, and she may seem like she wants to be left alone (this can result in being left to fend for herself far too often) but she *needs* nurturing—in the form of food, understanding, safety, and advice. She needs these things as much as your non-AS children, if not more so, but may get less attention because of her solitary ways. Don't let this happen.

She has enough confusion in her life already. Blame and guilt should not be part of the legacy that she carries for they most assuredly will result in other, psychological conditions (autism is neurological, not psychological, as many still think). These, in turn, may obscure AS and cause doctors and therapists to treat the symptoms rather than addressing the source.

Your daughter's battle with sensory issues, social issues and prejudice may be life-long. Give her a good start by embracing her idiosyncrasies, even if she doesn't like it when you embrace her physically.

6

GENDER ROLES
AND IDENTITY

Gender roles have annoyed me since puberty, when all my childhood girlfriends started paying more attention to their looks than to books and started acting nicer to boys than they did to me. Since then they have bothered me in ways too numerous to list. Whether it is the fact that all commercials for cleaning products feature women and that every single movie trailer has a male voice-over, I have issues with society's assumptions and reinforcing stereotypes.

Splitting AS traits along gender lines may seem unnecessary to many on the spectrum because we tend to be androgynous creatures—in mannerisms, behavior and, mostly, in essence.

> I think gender roles are a load of BS. I didn't understand gender when I was young, and had issues with bullying because of it... I don't understand femininity. In my mind, stereotypical women seem boring, petty, materialistic, and completely irrational. I'd rather be interesting and outcast. (Andi)

Our androgyny shines through our feminine shells. Many times I've been accused of being either a transvestite or a lesbian and that has also happened to my Aspergirl peers.

In high school, girls treated me like I was something else, not boy, not girl, just an *it*. (Elfinia)

In my mind, in my self-perception, I have a male identity as well as a female one and can visually picture my male self.

I have never felt female or able to be "one of the girls."
I actually feel as if I am half male and half female. (Camilla)

I discovered that, in fact, most if not *all* Aspergirls have similar perceptions about gender. Our anima and animus seem to be of equal influence and power. For some it manifests in obvious ways—being the breadwinner in a relationship, or allowing children to live with their father while she pursues her career. For others it manifests sexually; although most of the Aspergirls are heterosexual, a substantial number said that their partner's gender didn't matter. Mostly it manifests as frustration, and disinterest in society's expectations at what being female means. As usual, we march to our own drum.

I was probably seven when I was one shot from beating a boy at table hockey. I saw the look on his face that he could lose to a girl. I scored. I have never backed down from a guy. Nevertheless, females do not make much sense to me. When one plays with girly-girls, heaven only knows what the game is about—I certainly never figured it out. (Widders)

Though we may not feel particularly womanly, others will still see us as such and measure our behavior against nonautistic females, when in reality I feel it would be more appropriate and fair to measure our behavior against a man's—after all, men are not expected to be socially adept, or have an abundance of nurturing feelings. This would be a much fairer standard of measure and other Aspergirls agree.

> Women are typically measured by how well they can multi-task, regulate their impulses, smooth over conflict and soothe other people's emotions. People say women are equal to men, but they still expect women to carry far more of the burden for other people's happiness than they are conscious of or care to admit—this magnifies ridiculously for spectrum women. (Stella)

Another aspect to being a woman is the amount of grooming we may be expected to do. I once read that the average female spends thousands of hours of her life—hundreds of days—*getting ready* to go out. That just seems silly to us. While *basic* hygiene is not a gender issue, how "decorated" society expects us to be *is*—makeup, hair products, lotions, potions, etc. We'll talk more about that in Chapter 8.

> I will never buy lots and lots of shoes. I have no understanding why anyone needs that many shoes, or would even want them. Makeup makes me want to claw my face off, I can't/won't wear it. (Elfinia)

It's not just gender identity that we may struggle with—it's identity in general. It does seem to be a trend, for some of us, to have a changeable personality either based on our current role model, or changing interests.

> I have exhibited that well documented chameleon-like nature that is spoken of in relation to women with AS. I do not have a clear or typical sense of self. (Camilla)

Are we just impressionable or are we true *chameleons*? Does this changeability stem from a mind hungry to experience life from many angles, a dissatisfaction with who we are, or really just not knowing who we are? When I was a child I wanted to see, be, and do as much as I possibly could. I read and later traveled voraciously to seek this out. I remember that I always felt like an empty vessel that needed to be filled with experiences so that

I could craft an identity out of them. Other people, throughout my life, seemed like they already had identities and therefore, seemingly, had less need for experiences.

I even picked up accents quickly, as if searching for an ethnic identity as well. I was once fired from a hostess job in New York. I picked up a Hispanic accent from talking to kitchen staff and the boss thought I was an illegal immigrant. When I lived in England, I had a full-fledged British accent.

Alien to our gender, to our culture...and to our species? The term *alien* has often been used to describe the Aspergian experience. Some of us felt not only like we weren't particularly female as children but also like we were not from the same planet as everyone else. This is a good part of the reason so many of us love sci-fi and fantasy. The books of C.S. Lewis and J.R.R. Tolkien gave me hope that there were other worlds, places where I would fit in. The very first record I bought was "Space Oddity" by David Bowie. I related to his character, his persona, although I was only six years old at the time. I felt like I was literally in the wrong world and particularly in the wrong family; that there had been some sort of terrible mistake. And I am by no means the only Aspergirl who feels this way—virtually every single one of them said that they never felt that they "fit in."

> I still love X-Men. When I was younger, thinking of myself as being like one of the mutants (without the super powers) made me feel like even though I was different, I could live with others. (Dame Kev)

ADVICE TO ASPERGIRLS

Most of us don't really need any advice in the gender department, just validation...our anima/animus seem pretty balanced and that is something to be proud of. If kids make fun of you, just know we've all been there, and the kinds of kids who make fun of us in school usually end up right where they started—same place, same mentality. People who really know who they are, are lucky in some ways, but they are perhaps less challenged to grow. We have a thirst for knowledge; our personalities will develop if we don't hold ourselves back.

If our sense of who we are changes with our interest, maybe being a chameleon *is* our nature. I do believe that we each have core identities which will run throughout our lives, no matter what externals change. Each woman that I interviewed for this book had a distinct voice and character and it was easy for me to see that they had strong personalities even if they can't see that themselves all the time.

As far as identity and what is normal, everything that constitutes society is a construct. I learned that in Sociology 101 (Basic Sociology) but I saw it firsthand when I traveled around the world. What's polite in one place is offensive in another. Some cultures read right to left and back to front. While there is no Asperger homeland, no mother ship, that means to a large extent we are free to create our own culture, our own rules, and our own environment. As one Aspergirl, "Stella," said, "Barring anything dangerous or unsanitary, do whatever it takes to cope."

It is important to identify for yourself some core values, and to look to a higher source to find them—whatever that means to you. It may be a superhero or it may be a religious figure. It may be a character from a book. We learn social behavior by emulation. To look at the popular kids and try to act like them means that we might find ourselves with a whole new set of behaviors and morals that are not our own. Choose wisely.

ADVICE TO PARENTS

Dads, the great thing about having an AS daughter is she will be more likely to want to help you fix the car and build a fort than help Mom cook dinner. This is a trait that may be overlooked because she's in her head so much and is so solitary much of the time.

Being a goofy but intellectual tomboy is normal in our world. Similarly, if she wants to decorate her room like Rivendell and can't get her nose out of her fantasy books, understand she feels that she doesn't fit in with this world. Who's to say why this is? As the saying goes, we are in this world, but we don't have to be "of it." This world is not of our making, so it's no wonder we want and need to make our own.

This can result in a type of restlessness, a craving for experience and identity. It could result in lots of stops and starts, whether in the areas of employment, education, or even geographic location. If you daughter seems to be losing herself, she's probably emulating…again, this is normal, but if she's behaving in a way that is inconsistent with her usual code of conduct and ethics, you might want to find the source and help her replace it with a more appropriate role model.

7

PUBERTY AND MUTISM

This is a book about females, so you will no doubt expect me to talk about periods. To be honest it didn't occur to me to do so at first. They are a biological function that necessarily inconveniences all women, not just Aspergirls. I asked around and nobody really cared enough to talk about them. But they are important for a couple of reasons. They throw our body chemistry into turmoil. Some Aspergirls don't really show strong autistic symptoms until puberty. Prior to this we may just seem gifted; but when puberty hits, it flips us on our heads and you can see our autistic underbelly.

Periods do throw up more hurdles on an already difficult terrain fraught with social hazards and budding acne. And because we may not have friends, we won't have anyone to talk to about it and so we don't really understand what's going on. Those turgid movies they used to show at school make us feel embarrassed and don't actually describe very well what periods are for.

> When I grew up there were sex ed classes but looking back they were very basic and really didn't address the fact that we (human beings) are physically primed for reproduction. (Tina)

Society doesn't really give us the straight talk either—periods are made to seem weird and creepy. Menstruation is biological but it's been given religious and moral connotations which confuse us. In western culture a woman's period used to be called her "curse," because of the Christian belief that it started when God punished Eve for her sin. This gives females a fair amount of shame just for having healthy reproduction organs necessary for perpetuating the species. Aspergirls, being literal creatures, may take that shame on board.

> Anytime I had to change a pad at school my face would get very red. I felt like everyone knew my secret even though probably no one did. I felt intense shame and guilt for something that's just natural. (Elfinia)

Bringing tampons/pads to school and making sure we change them is a whole new routine; a potential logistical nightmare complicated by cramps. We don't like being scrutinized—when we have our periods, we feel like everyone else can tell and it's humiliating for us. We may obsess that we're leaking and want to raise our hand every five minutes to go to the toilet—you get the idea. There may be shame and embarrassment over body functions in general. Even going pee when there are others in adjacent stalls, just blowing our noses, can feel like something shameful and horrifying. How much so will have a lot to do with our parents and how much information we are given to prepare and demystify things for us. And how open others in our household are.

Another difference between high-functioning girls and nonautistics is that the nonautistic may welcome periods as a sign of budding womanhood, and the Aspergirl may see it as an unwelcome intrusion into her childhood—or personhood.

It is about this same time that we may begin to suffer *selective mutism*, or that mutism episodes may increase in intensity and frequency. Mutism is triggered by severe social anxiety; a verbal manifestation of our "deer in the headlights" reaction to social contact. Actions such as freezing during danger are controlled by the amygdala, which we know is stimulated in people with Asperger's by other people. Where neurotypicals see safety in numbers, we see threat.

Virtually every Aspergirl I interviewed experienced selective mutism at some point in her life, and some still experience it. This occasional inability to speak strikes the minds and tongues of both males with Asperger's and Aspergirls, and it is very unpleasant for all, but girls are "expected" to be socially competent creatures. When was the last time you heard the term "still waters run deep" applied to a female? A woman who cannot speak when spoken to will just seem overly shy or unfriendly; perhaps she will even appear mentally challenged. In a culture which currently seems to prize confidence over substance, this extremely public illustration of our shyness and withdrawal is very embarrassing and isolating.

> There are plenty of times when my brain freezes and I don't figure out what to say for a few days or so afterwards—my ability to continue the conversation just shuts down, and I'm restricted to rehearsed statements that add nothing. (Anemone)

> It used to happen an awful lot when I was a kid. If someone was angry I would be unable to respond. Very large painful lump in my throat, metallic taste. Would be entirely unable to speak. (Sam)

Mutism not only hijacks our words but also our ability to think. To use the "needle on the record" analogy, the needle gets stuck on the same unpleasant lyric, and we can't shake it free to move on to the next line.

> I am able to think but it's very slowed. I very much want to speak but cannot. It feels as though the neural pathways are racing to process the traffic jam on the information

highway and because it is overloaded with information the roads start to clog. So the road of language is the first to shut down. Eventually I am able to speak again, but slowly. It takes time to get the traffic flowing at an even pace again. (Brandi)

Mutism first struck me at home, when I was a young girl. My house was filled with dysfunction, sometimes violence, and erratic, unhappy feelings much of the time. Around my siblings I sometimes could not speak for a couple of days at a time, maybe longer, but they didn't seem to notice or to care; they were embroiled in their own dramas. School had been something of a sanctuary for me until the bullying started and then there was no place safe to go—my beloved fields and woods had been decimated by apartment complexes and shopping malls. Mutism reached crisis level with the onset of puberty—whenever I was around older kids from my school, or bullies, and especially at social gatherings—i.e. where there was no structure or purpose. Everyone else seemed to be so relaxed and to know what to say to each other, like they'd each been given a script and I was the only one who had to adlib. It was very confusing for me. If I was in a rare confident mood, I could perform or bluff my way through. Usually I was not. I'd begin by feeling uncomfortable, sense that maybe I wasn't fitting in. I might feel a little hostility coming from someone. Discomfort intensified and then a paralysis would steal over my limbs. It would strike my ability to speak and all my other motor skills—my movements would become very jerky and stiff. My thoughts too, would freeze—I would think over and over "They don't like me." As people conversed with each other, my lack of participation, instead of helping me to become invisible, which is what I wanted, only made me stand out like a beacon of social ineptitude. I couldn't get up and leave, for often I was physically frozen to the spot. Their gaze would land on me more and more, like a searchlight. Sometimes, they'd just look quizzical—What's this girl's problem? I felt like Captain von Trapped, without the benefit of a stone to hide behind. They'd always find me; ask a direct question, forcing me to speak. By this time, I could only utter a monotone, monosyllabic grunt, or maybe repeat something one of the other girls had said. Or worse, I'd laugh, which at this point was more like a creepy giggle. The thoughts in my head moved from "They don't like me" to self-scolding: "Cut it out, relax, what's wrong with you?" Unfortunately, once it started, it didn't quit until I was away from whatever person or environment triggered it, until I was alone again or with a close friend. Then it would dissipate, slowly and painfully. It invariably damaged *all* my friendships because even a best friend gets tired of you acting weird and embarrassing yourself, and them by association. The experience always left me feeling horrible; depressed, flawed, even suicidal—I remember sticking my head in a gas oven for a few seconds at a very young age. I didn't know what was wrong with me and why other kids didn't seem to experience this. Even kids I considered geeks— far less cool than me—could speak and joke and smile when in these groups. The feeling mutism gave me was one of deep embarrassment, shame and alienation.

> This weekend I was invited out by friends/acquaintances but the whole time my selective mutism was on. I didn't have any words to say unless they asked me a specific question; even then it was a challenge not to stutter. (Elle)

> When put on the spot, or in an intense situation, I seize up and can't get words to form a sentence. It is the most frustrating thing in the world. It puts a lot of strain on my relationships and does nothing good for self-esteem. (Bramble)

The feelings of paralysis during mutism got stronger and more frequent until I finally entered a phase where I would actually pass right out. According to Dr. Stephen Edelson of the Center for Autism (2009), about one in four spectrum kids will begin to suffer seizures during the onset of puberty. Most of the seizures will be subclinical, not the obvious convulsive variety. Subclinical seizures could be the possible cause of underlying selective mutism. I distinctly felt that I was not getting enough oxygen to my brain. Once I started passing out, even my mother had to take notice; I was given a brain scan which revealed nothing, but subclinical seizures are not detectable by an ordinary EEG (electroencephalogram: a test to detect problems in the electrical activity of the brain).

In those days, kids didn't see shrinks and nothing at all was done about it. Around this time, a relative who had shown special interest in me, proclaimed that I was growing up badly and removed herself from my life. (I believe she was an over-privileged Aspergirl who needed a little work in the empathy department.) I was left alone, with undiagnosed Asperger's, neighborhood kids/schoolmates who frightened me, oblivious teachers and a dysfunctional family. I was on the threshold of puberty. I couldn't talk properly, walk properly (I swung my arms wildly), had perpetually greasy hair, and I didn't think like everyone else. I wasn't normal. Needless to say, life was hell, and mutism was the devil—the absolute worse aspect of childhood and growing up. I simply do not relate to people who have had a happy childhood. I don't begrudge them, I envy them.

> Mutism is actually my biggest problem. It always has been. I have a difficult time speaking fluently as it is, because my brain doesn't work in words. It works in images, sounds, patterns. When I'm upset or nervous my translation system breaks down. I can think and think and think, but I can't turn any of it into words—and I can't exactly project my thoughts out through my forehead. It hurts, and it hurts others when I can't respond to them. (Andi)

The drugs don't work: One of the paths I took to correcting my social awkwardness and my mutism was drink and drugs. I tried this alternative route in my early teens, to see if I could "free my mind" and experience the world differently; perhaps this was a way to blend in with everyone else in my neighborhood. Drugs did nothing for my social skills. In fact, they made them worse. My mutism episodes and fainting spells increased. Aspergirls and parents be warned—we are far too sensitive mentally and physically to engage in "recreational" drugs. They can be very deleterious to our health and well-being.

On the rare occasion that I was actually able to relax and speak at a gathering I was always very happy and excited inside...and relieved. To this day when I feel intimidated by someone it impacts my ability to comprehend their words— which sound garbled and nonsensical. In turn, my own ability to communicate is impeded and my thinking becomes foggy and slow. I now use this as a sort of radar—although I'm learning to socialize with a broader scope of people, those who affect me in this way are generally not people I want to be around very much. Kind, open and non-judgmental people do not "mutate" me as I like to call it, and these are the people I do want to be around. I've heard it said by many others with Asperger's/ autism, that we have a sixth sense, perhaps to compensate for, or as an alternative to, normal awareness. I think I have a "meanie detector," and when it senses there's a meanie in the room, it tells me not to speak to them. Of course, I'm learning that it doesn't have to be me that should shut up.

> The mutism lasted until my mid-20s. Unfamiliar or judgmental people would trigger it and it would last as long as I was with those people. When I have selective mutism, I cannot form a novel thought and it is like blackness. (Widders)

Mutism is not the same as a lack of interest in reciprocal conversation. That is voluntary, mutism is not.

Off medication I do not talk, except to monologue at others about my interests. I find the reciprocity of conversation to be tiring and hard to follow. I stay most days on my own with my own thoughts. (Camilla)

ADVICE TO ASPERGIRLS

Periods are an annoyance but they are completely natural, not a curse from God as some would have us think. We are the perpetuators of the species, should we choose to be, and that is what periods are for. All of your body functions are natural—sneezing, pooping and anything else you might feel embarrassed about. Cramps can be crippling—Midol is a simple effective way to control cramping, as is yoga, massage, and exercise in general. Keep a journal of your periods so that you can predict them and be ready. Keep tampons in your locker. Don't worry, no one can tell. Do realize however, we get a bit stinkier during our period, so if for example you don't normally use deodorant, you might want to at this time, and be sure to shower regularly.

Selective mutism is horrible, it feels like a seizure even if it isn't, and there's a sort of hangover feeling afterward—it's not just something that quickly comes and goes. No matter what the neurological process is, the source is social/emotional—lack of confidence and being uncomfortable or intimidated. I do think we are supersensitive and pick up vibes from people and if we pick up something negative, it shuts us down. The trick is twofold: increase your self-confidence, and also, seek out the good in others—find whatever aspect of them you resonate with, not against. This is most difficult when you're a teenager, when life is a minefield of judgment and raging chemicals—from without as well as within.

We need to practice speaking, in speech therapy, clubs, special interest groups, phone calls, strangers in supermarkets… we just need to practice talking. I'm not saying that we need to stoop to "How about those Yankees?" but anything to keep the flow going. You'll get better with practice. Get an education to increase your social circle, range of interests, and body of knowledge, and to get the job you want so that you are around like-minded people.

Reciprocal conversation skills can be improved. Most conversation should be like a relaxed game of tennis, not solitaire with one player and one spectator. That will be fun for the player and tedious for the watcher. Try really learning to listen while others are speaking and not worrying about what you're going to say next.

Unlike other people who seem to be on fairly solid ground in social situations, we're on a tightrope and it doesn't take much for us to lose our balance. Our ability to overcome and manage mutism will be affected by our overall health, mental health, happiness, and diet. Remember that overall good health is not just absence of disease, it means being physically fit.

You will probably grow out of this mutism before adulthood, or it will at least diminish in frequency and scope. Your powerlessness to speak comes from confusion, not knowing what to say and having self-doubt; everything bottlenecks in the brain and also in the throat—like a clogged drain. While it is happening, don't beat yourself up mentally (or abuse yourself physically). It will pass, I promise. If you are in a place where you are not comfortable, for example a party, then leave if you can safely do so. Go home, put on your favorite music, cuddle your kitten or soft toy, write down your thoughts. If you have someone to talk to, do so once you can speak again.

Many of you do have someone that "gets" you. But even those of you that don't, you still have paper and pen or a PC. Write. Writing has saved my sanity if not my life and the lives of countless Aspergirls I've spoken to. It will validate your thoughts—you will read them later with a clear head and you will see that much of what you think is reasonable and true. Some of it will be quite negative—in those cases you need to re-frame what you are looking at and what you are thinking about. Think of our psyches as colored lenses—sometimes we see everything in grey, sometimes the same view is rosy. You have some control over what lens you look through, but it takes focus and discipline which you have in abundance.

If you don't write, then use your medium—art, dance, music, etc.

ADVICE TO PARENTS

It is important that your daughter be told about periods before they happen and given practical instruction, or the sight of blood emanating from her body will terrify her. It will be especially difficult for her if she is withdrawn at home, because she can't or won't tell you what is going on with herself, so she may be struggling with this "horrible" incident on her own. She may have a lot of shame about all her body functions. Being open about this kind of stuff will help her to feel more comfortable with her body functions. It's probably best not to use euphemisms like "curse" or "rag" because with her literal mind, she'll see that as derogatory and something to be ashamed of. Just give her the scientific facts—your uterus fills with blood three weeks of the month and during the fourth week it needs to empty itself. No big deal.

When your Aspergirl is quiet it may be that she has nothing to say. It may be she is lost in her own thoughts. But if there is an actual inability to speak or move that is another thing entirely. There is a paralysis happening that must have been brought on by something—some event, some words, something. Ask your daughter to write a journal when this is going on to see if you can discover the various triggers—usually stress from new or unfriendly people.

While she may seem as if, or say, she wants to be alone, it can be a hellish experience and she needs to know you care even if she doesn't want you in the room. It will be embarrassing for her. Let her know you are not judging her, that other girls with Asperger's go through the exact same thing. That her powerlessness is temporary and has both a physical cause and a solution.

I'll reiterate that I think we are supersensitive and just pick up vibes from people and if we pick up something negative, it shuts us down. This happens most frequently in the teenage years, when life is a minefield of judgment and you are always surrounded by peers. You also have less control over your environment when young. Respect her need for privacy and quiet while letting her know you are there for her.

8

ATTRACTION, DATING, SEX, AND RELATIONSHIPS

We have a marvelous ability to think about things in depth, continually, for long periods of time. In our hobbies, it's called *passion*. At work or school, it's called *focus*. But in our personal life, it's called *obsession*. It's all the same Aspie trait. It's okay to be obsessed with inanimate objects or information, but to be obsessed with people is dangerous, particularly if they are not mutually interested. We, and our doctors and parents, have to understand that we are obsessive creatures and this might be a component of our relationships to watch out for. It is true that some Aspergirls are not interested in romance at all. But since we are emotionally naïve, very sense-oriented, have a lack of understanding of gender roles, and a fight-or-flight reaction to others, if we *are* romantically inclined, you might get a girl who chases boys with a dreamy idea of romance who can't actually stand to *have* a boyfriend.

> I've never had any success with men I'm very attracted to, never! I end up seen as a stalker. I've learned you don't call a guy 12 times a night to see if he's home and talk to him every night, but I still don't seem to know what's appropriate. (Elfinia)

When I was 12 I obsessed over one of the coolest, best-looking boys in the neighborhood. He was 17. Being sensory-driven, I could not stop myself from staring at his hair and eyes. One day, he was sitting behind me on a sofa and I was sitting on the floor in front of the television (we were all watching a movie) and every few seconds I'd turn my head around 180 degrees to look at him. He avoided my gaze and merely smirked. I'm sure there were plenty of *Exorcist* jokes after I left. I distinctly remember not being able to stop myself. I also remember thinking that no one would notice, but of course they did, how could they not? I was in front of everyone. But I lacked theory of mind—if I couldn't see myself, how could others see me? I also believed that if I loved him, he must love me. After chasing him obsessively for months, he finally rebuked me in an angry, almost frightened voice, "You're not a girl, I don't know *what* you are." That was the first time that I realized that something about me could scare people, but I still couldn't fathom what I'd done wrong.

Girls are "supposed" to play hard to get, but Aspergirls don't play games. Besides not understanding gender roles and expectations, we are logical, direct creatures. We may think things like "I want to go out with him; therefore I should ask him out," and set ourselves up for ridicule and rejection. The whole process of dating and what to do and how to do it is beyond most of us. We try and fail to behave in a way that attracts dates. We may be rejected frequently because of our inappropriate behavior, both in high school and as adults. We may become very afraid of rejection and avoid anything to do with romance as a result. A life-long love affair with solitude may begin here.

> I don't ever want a boyfriend or have anything to do with romantic anything. (Megan)

> Mostly, I'm afraid of men, so when one pays attention to me, my radar goes full-active. In general I tend to be relieved when I become aware that he is not someone I

need to take seriously (i.e. be afraid of). Then I can just relax and take him as he is. (Anemone)

In addition to not knowing what to do, as far as dating a new person, we have to worry about their reaction to the more extreme obvious signs of AS, such as mutism and meltdowns. Even more subtle displays of AS traits, such as bluntness or monologuing, might cause a date to wonder.

> In high school I had lots of friends but not many dates. My random panic attacks in public made me un-date-worthy. (Dame Kev)

> For any kind of close relationship to form I have to trust the other person won't be offended by my various quirks, for example if I need to leave a party before I meltdown in public. (Stella)

Social withdrawal, quiet fear and confusion about our own bodies, selective mutism, awkwardness, tics, lack of reciprocal conversation skills, limits our choice of partner. Society prizes confidence and appearance and we just don't seem very confident. We might also neglect our appearance. We may not realize that our hair is frizzily out of fashion. We know there are metals in antiperspirants and chemicals in skin and hair products which are not good for us, but we don't realize that because we don't use them, we may look plain and even be a bit smelly. This doesn't make us too attractive to others. We have to find our own easy-to-maintain style, and natural products that bring out our best.

Fortunately, all it really takes is one person to "get us." Another Aspie perhaps, or at least someone eccentric. Someone who knows we're quirky and likes us because of it, not in spite of it. And someone whom we can trust not to hold our traits against us.

We went to art school together, that's how we got to know each other. We didn't start dating right away. He asked me out, but I was so surprised I said no at first. (Riley)

I have known my partner since we were four years old and we were a couple in primary school! He knows more about AS than me and he's very aware about how to handle my meltdowns or upsets in life. (Sarah)

Relationships with other people is where we are most out of our element, so we may not realize it when someone is treating us badly or we may think that it comes with the territory. When we're younger we may settle for anyone, just to have someone—we may just be surprised and pleased that someone wants us. Because we can't always get the type of person we want, we often let our first partners choose us; we may not be very discriminating.

Partners seem to choose me and I'm too flattered by being noticed to make a reasonable decision. I feel like I could love anyone, they just have to be nice to me. (Bramble)

Many of us can have partners more easily than friends. As Aspergirls, we need some control over our environment, and you can influence a boyfriend (leverage compliance) with regard to sensory and social issues. But we are still easy targets for abusers and Svengali-type partners, the ones who sense that we might be easy to mold or manipulate.

When I was younger I let myself stay in a somewhat controlling and sexually abusive relationship because I didn't know how to stand up for myself. I was made to feel like everything I thought was automatically wrong, because I lacked the seemingly automatic knowledge that other people seemed to have of what was and was not acceptable. (Olive)

The potentially serious consequences of this are in stark contrast to our seeming intelligence—getting pregnant too early, contracting a sexually transmitted disease (STD), being left with children to raise on our own, or being emotionally and sexually unfulfilled. Half the time we don't know we're unfulfilled because we have nothing to compare it with. The people around us will often shake their heads in despair, wondering how such smart women could make such bad choices when it comes to relationships.

Even shared interests, while a good criterion for friends, is not enough of a platform for a relationship. Just because you both love the same type of music, for example, doesn't mean that he is going to be good to you.

Because of emotional naïveté, and a passion for books and films, some of us have a very Walt Disney view of romance, and have had our heads filled with stories which might not paint the most realistic picture of what relationships are. It's nice to be idealistic, but without discrimination, we frequently end up hurt.

> I start at the beginning of the relationship giving the guy the benefit of the doubt, treating him as if he could be "the one." The fallout is frequent disappointment and depression. My therapist, friends, etc. tell me that I should "interview" the guy further, make him prove himself, so I do this more now. (Ann Marie)

Some Aspergirls figure out that they're vulnerable but can't work out how *not* to be, so they avoid sex and relationships altogether.

> I have not been in a real sexual relationship. Being pretty and gullible I've had too many guys try to force me into

things. As a result I'm very wary of getting physically involved. (Andi)

Our strong sensory issues cause us to be attracted to things like hair and eyes when we're young. When we're older we start to look for unusual personalities, such as other Aspies. When we're older and wiser, we try to find someone who encompasses all our needs. But senses will always play a big part for us—a man's smell ranked as being absolutely crucial to attraction for most Aspergirls.

> To be physically attracted they have to, how can I describe it… "smell" in the right way. A sniff at the neck of the right person and I'm lost—*if* we are on the same intellectual level. But these components are rarely found in the same man, so I have had only two men in my life. (Siv)

Sexual activity is strongly affected if not determined by sensory issues—because of them, some Aspergirls love sex and it is an extremely intense, pleasurable experience. But the majority of Aspergirls I interviewed did not like sex because of those same sensory issues—it was either too painful or just plain annoying. As a result, many were celibate by choice, while others had sex mainly because their husband or partner wanted it.

> I enjoy sex very much, more than my friends. I think my heightened senses make it more enjoyable. (Ann Marie)

> Sex hurts too much; no partner for a long time. (Anemone)

> I'm happy if it makes my husband happy. There is too much happening for me to relax, even after 30 years with the same partner. (Pokégran)

> I haven't had sex in seven years. I've always had this push/pull thing. I may want a guy, but I'm scared to have them actually touch me. (Elfinia)

Because of a lack of interest in pursuing and maintaining relationships some will forgo sex even though they might enjoy it.

> I have never had sex, and never plan to. I have had a total of one date in my entire life. I also had a brief online relationship with an Aspie male. I find myself neglecting relationships, and it only leads to other people getting hurt. (Shannon)

Having a relationship mean risking a breakup, which is never easy but can be particularly difficult for Aspergirls. We have let ourselves be vulnerable, we've let someone in, and we've allowed a new routine to take root. We have these naïve ideas of love—we're thinking "forever" and he's thinking "for a while."

> There was a lot of heartache and tears when I would have a breakup after a long relationship…a big meltdown because I had to rearrange my routine to not have that boyfriend (or girlfriend) in it. (Dame Kev)

Other authors have pointed out that AS males tend to date or marry older women, but in our case, I've noticed a trend for us to date or marry younger men. In many cases, this does work out—because we act, feel, and often appear younger than our chronological age it's logical we'd get along with younger males. However, it is possible we may set ourselves up for disappointment. For example, if you are 34 and you are dating a 22-year-old, you might get along very well, but he might not be ready for the kind of commitment you are hoping for.

While it is difficult to find a nurturing partner, if we have not been diagnosed, we will be difficult in turn. I think that not knowing I had AS sabotaged all of my relationships to some extent. In all honesty, throughout my life I was not what you'd call low-maintenance. I was moody, temperamental, and prone to terrifying rage meltdowns as well as man-repelling depression meltdowns. I was hypersensitive, constantly overloaded, lacked theory of mind, was blunt, self-absorbed, and rigid in thought and behavior. In my defense, I will say also that I was passionate, loyal, honest, and idealistic. But I was naïve. I had strong romantic and physical cravings without the capacity to make good decisions about a man.

Most of us have not had a best girlfriend since high school. That puts a lot of weight on a boyfriend to be best friend as well as lover. If we have difficulty maintaining employment and are often in financial crisis mode, he may also be our provider, which doesn't fly too far in this modern world. If we don't want a social life, we may be happy sitting home every night watching *Hamlet* or *Sense and Sensibility* for the trillionth time, but he may not be. Whether he's NT or AS, he'll have his own agenda. It is accurate to say that you must find someone to accept you for who you are, but if you don't know who you are, then they can't possibly, can they? We must be aware of our deficits to make and attract a good partner. That is what I was saying in *22 Things a Woman Must Know If She Loves a Man with Asperger's Syndrome* (Simone 2009) and it stands equally true for us women on the spectrum.

Disclosure is always a choice and a crossroad. With it, we risk losing someone before they have a chance to know us. But without it, we give them no frame of reference for understanding. We may cause new partners confusion and worry; hurt feelings and a damaged or aborted relationship. For this reason, many women tell me that they would only date someone on the spectrum; or at least, someone who is very tolerant and a bit eccentric. There are distinct advantages to having a spectrum partner, but one good thing about a non-spectrum partner is that he can do many of the things that perhaps you cannot— remember long strings of verbal instructions, make smalltalk at social events while you just smile and look enigmatic—it can be nice to know that someone is picking up your slack. Of course, he will run to you whenever he's trying to figure out some new software, so it will most definitely be a symbiotic relationship.

But he needs to be someone who has a good sense of humor, is intelligent, and very understanding of all the issues we contend with.

ADVICE TO ASPERGIRLS

If a guy can't handle it when you talk about quantum physics, Manga, or Dungeons and Dragons, then he probably isn't the guy for you. If he gets embarrassed by your bluntness, you're probably not a good match. If he doesn't get your jokes, references, etc., then do you really want to pursue it? We tend to feel flawed and want to change ourselves to be accepted. We are good mimics and we think that we can mimic being the kind of girl that guys will like. By all means work on yourself, but most important, *be* yourself. Don't dumb yourself down. Revel in your uniqueness. Be proud of your intelligence, your faculty with words. Celebrate geek power. You might not even be a geek, once you see that smarts are sexy. Maybe you're not awkward, just lacking in confidence. *Anyone can get a stylist. Not everyone can get an intellect.* Your uniqueness will eventually translate into a personal style that is the real you. That is how you will find a partner that truly connects with you. You may never be the most popular girl in school. I was voted the "worst" girl in my high school (at an informal but very large gathering in the boys' bathroom) and I know it hurts. But if you are genuine and pursue your own interests, that is how you will connect with your soul mates—whether friends, colleagues or romantic partners.

Instead of spending a lot of time and energy trying to make some guy you are attracted to like you, go out with someone who already *does* like you. That will save time and heartache. Believe it or not, this is something single people of all ages and neuro-persuasions need to hear. Remember too that if the kind of guy you want doesn't seem to notice you, you might want to ask yourself if you are making the most of what nature gave you. Many of us, including myself, think that spending a lot of money and time on our appearance is illogical and stupid, but if we think of it as the "uniform" to getting the job (i.e. the relationship) then we might be more inclined to put it on. When I'm writing, and there's no one around, I can go days wearing the same bathrobe, without makeup or brushing my hair (I know, ick!) but I want to keep my current partner interested. So I will make an effort to keep the package pretty. It's not nearly as important as what's on the inside, but men are very visual creatures and all the protesting in the world is not going to change that. This advice applies to anything we want in life. Our appearance needs to match the genre, job, subculture, etcetera, that we want to accept us and that we want to be part of.

A lot of us have begun to mistrust the chemicals they put in soaps, shampoos, lotions, and hair dyes as well as perfumes. Long before we knew we were Aspie we had an aversion to these things and reactions ranging from rashes to headaches. As a result we use very few products and are selective and faithful when we find something we like. We can become slightly immune to our own smell so it is probably a good idea to make or buy a natural alternative rather than, say, not showering or washing our hair altogether. There are also metal-free deodorants and organic natural scents if you seek them out. Again thank god for the internet, because we can go on forums and find out what others are doing and hear about stores and sites that sell products we can use or get tips from other Aspergirls.

We have a need for control and this can carry over into our relationships. If we like a guy we may call him, ask him out, etc. and unless he too has Asperger's or is extremely liberated that may not be the best thing to do in the long run. It may turn him off. You are not an NT girl, but you still are a female and society is still more traditional than it likes to think it is. Men and boys are still "supposed" to be the ones to call (not *my* rules—I despise gender roles). And in your case, you might get upset if he doesn't call back right away and that can lead to some obsessive re-calling.

To young Aspergirls

Let him know you like him, if you feel safe to do so, with a smile and a brief friendly word from time to time. But when a guy you like doesn't "get" you, he just isn't right for you, no matter how good he smells and no matter how blue his eyes and silky his hair! If you find yourself sailing into obsessive behavior, turn that boat around. That is okay when dealing with inanimate objects, books, or knowledge, but when dealing with another human being, it is dangerous and could be both frightening and disturbing to them. It could sabotage a potential relationship and could also get you a reputation. Know that you are not operating from an informed place. We may have an attraction to his quirks, his eccentricities (especially if he has AS too) or simply his hair, eyes, and five o'clock shadow. We need to remind ourselves that: a) we don't know him very well at all, and b) life is not a Jane Austen novel. Informed thought-out choices are the best ones as opposed to "love at first sight" for an Aspergirl, simply because we don't read others' intentions all that well at first, and we may take longer to get to know someone. Ideally we must try to take our time.

When you do meet someone you like and who likes you, early disclosure may be the way to go. When I started dating my partner he knew from my work that I had Asperger's. He realized that he needed to read about it and take the information on board if he was going to be with me. That suited me just fine. I did not want the task of trying to be "normal'—I'm just not up for that. He now knows almost as much about it as I do and can anticipate sensory and emotional challenges. Men can be great caretakers and very sensitive—just because we're women doesn't mean we have to do all the emotional work!

If you don't want to go for full disclosure, you can still state your needs so that he doesn't take you to the wrong type of place or function for your first date. For example, if you're invited to a party you can say that you'd prefer to go somewhere a bit quieter so you can get to know each other a bit and talk. If *that* raises his eyebrows, then he's not the guy for you at this time.

We have to figure out what our needs are before we can have them met. Some want reassurance from a partner; some don't need it and are happy just being contacted twice a week and being left alone the rest of the time. Love might not be as lovey-dovey as we'd hoped and fantasized about. We may still have an urge to flee the room, dislike holding hands, not want to see him more than once or twice per week. This will conflict with our expectations. We may ask ourselves "What's wrong with me? Why don't I want to be with him more often?" And we might even throw a positive relationship out the window because we are experiencing some of this stuff. While the right person will not affect us as negatively or push our autistic buttons as often as the wrong one, they are still another human being and so we will still have to retreat and recharge, even from Mr. (or Ms.) Wonderful. We think that "the One" will not have this effect on us. To think that is erroneous and is essentially saying that the right partner will cure us of autism. He won't. You will still have stimulated amygdala that will make you want to flee sometimes, no matter what else he stimulates in you.

We are literal much of the time and need positive reinforcement. One problem with dating is that if we don't hear from the boy/man we may worry or wonder what he thinks of us. Don't judge a relationship or any situation by what is going on every single moment. It is normal when newly dating for him not to call you every day. It doesn't mean he doesn't like you or that he's not thinking of you. Here is a piece of advice my current amour gave me:

> You have a lot to offer someone but that will not happen if you give them a small window of time to perform to your expectations.

I found the window visual a very effective aid to keep me from worrying and wondering what other people think and from being tempted to fill in the blanks with my own thoughts, which sometimes spiral out of control in a downward trajectory. My partner adds this about our relationship:

> I'm learning a lot about Rudy's autism and how it is dealt with in regards to her and myself. Her fears equal isolation and she goes down the rabbit hole. Unlike you and I (nonautistics), she has difficulty stopping herself from hitting the bottom. Autistic people need very clear lines drawn. If any plan is waived they weave off the road. It's like a small fire that needs immediate attention or it will become a bigger one. Like any relationship, communication is the key and I'm still learning what she needs as someone with Asperger's.

Like many Aspergirls I didn't really set standards for myself prior to this current relationship, and I settled for men who were indifferent or cruel to me. I always tried to make the best of it and loved their good points, but being so tolerant is not a good thing if you are giving far more than you are receiving. I'd have been better off alone and indeed, I have spent many years of my adult life single.

Some Aspergirls are happy alone and start to wonder if there's something wrong with them when society puts pressure on and asks "Aren't you lonely?" It's nobody's business what you do, and if you are happy being alone, you are not flawed, you are lucky.

Be as pragmatic about romance as you are about other things in your life:

- Are you happy within yourself? Does he add to or detract from that happiness?

- Can you be yourself around him?

- Does he have something to offer that enhances your life and well-being?

- Have you worked on your style and appearance to make the most of what you've got and to reflect who you are?

As for sex, what you choose should be your choice and not society's. As long as there are consenting adults, "live and let live." If you feel that you are not getting as much out of sex as you could, and want to find out more, there are therapists, books, and videos and things you can do to explore your options.

Don't rush into sex because you think it's time you had it. Our first experience with something will leave an indelible mark. It should be with the right person, someone who knows and understands you and preferably someone who knows you have AS. We need and want to feel safe. If you have had an unpleasant or unsatisfying experience, know that sex with the right person can be infinitely different and more fulfilling.

Our awkward social skills can sometimes cause confusion. I was frequently accused of flirting throughout my life when I was just being friendly and practicing eye contact. Men can misread our intentions. While it is flattering to have someone want you, you do not have to reciprocate. Do not sleep with someone just because you have low self-esteem and it doesn't happen very often that someone wants you. Instead, work on loving yourself and figuring out what you need and want in a partner. It might take a while to find him or her but the experience will be worth the wait.

ADVICE TO PARENTS

Your daughter may have a hard time navigating romance. Try to find out if she is happy, lonely, etc. Encourage her to take care of her appearance and to integrate her own personal style and preferences with what is current, so she doesn't get picked on for looking too different. It's great to be counter-culture and unique to some extent, but going to school wearing floods (trousers that are too short) and two different shoes will just get her picked on. When we are younger a lot of us have a hard time remembering to wash our hair, put on makeup, or change our clothes. Most of us hate shopping. Give us help. Find out what role model's appearance or style she admires and is similar to; one that is relatively attainable to emulate. Get her a decent haircut and clothes. Remind her to groom—hair, nails, etc. She'll probably get better at that as she gets older but will still fall into slovenliness with depression episodes or when she's busy. She may not be what most people think of as a "girly" girl but she will thrive better with compliments and positive reinforcement.

Learn how to talk about sex a little. Let your daughter know that it is potentially a marvelous thing if and when the time and the person is right. If we do not get the support and understanding from you that we need, we will go into the world prematurely and will no doubt find ourselves in situations that we do not know how to handle and are not equipped to deal with. This can have grim consequences for an impressionable, emotionally naïve young girl—we often find ourselves at the mercy of men who do not have our best interests at heart. You must tell your Aspergirl that she is beautiful and worthy even if it doesn't seem that she cares to hear it or she will overreact to the slightest bit of sexual flattery.

Some parents have expressed concern that their daughter has unusual ideas about sex; for example visits porn sites, etc. Aspergirls are generally monogamous creatures. We are fairly conservative in our sex lives, if by mere fact of social shyness, though in our imaginations we may be a bit more adventurous. Don't worry that she is going to be a "wild thing." If you teach her to value herself it shouldn't be a problem.

9

FRIENDSHIPS
AND SOCIALIZING

I once saw a plaque in a British pub that said "Forget about our enemies. God save us from our friends!" Whoever said that must have been an Aspie. For we love our alone time. We love not having our peace wrecked by nonsensical conversation and meaningless activity. But at the same time, most of us also crave companionship and fun. It's complicated. People with Asperger's have a fight-or-flight reaction to all social contact. We want to be accepted for who we are but it is difficult to be yourself around others when you can't relax. Adrenalin kicks in, so if we don't run away, we might hog everyone's attention, do a little song-n-dance, or standup routine, then afterwards go home and have an after-party meltdown.

> I do not do social chit chat. Everything has a purpose and is about analysis. I do attend social gatherings occasionally but I pay with emotional overload and a meltdown or migraine the following day. (Camilla)

Because of this, and all the other myriad communication and sensory issues we contend with daily, we usually find friendships very difficult to maintain—and so we choose to fly solo. This plays out a little differently for Aspergirls than for our male counterparts—when was the last time you heard the phrase "lone wolf" applied to a female? Women who have no friends are simply weird, suspect—*cat ladies*. While it is plausible and acceptable for a man to be a loner, women are assumed and expected to be social creatures, arranging weekly margarita nights with girlfriends or having a phone surgically attached to our heads. According to the media and the myths of popular culture, girls can't even go to the bathroom alone, much less the mall. The reality is, whether we want them or not, most Aspergirls have few or no friends.

Our difficulties usually start in school. Other girls may make fun of us for our unfashionable looks and withdrawn or unusual mannerisms. Once you've been bullied, it gives you a glimpse into the darker side of human nature that other people may rarely, if ever, see. That is something you never quite forget, even if you learn to get along with people and see their good side later in life. It can prevent you from ever getting truly close to people, for you come to believe that what constitutes popularity is not something of any deep or lasting value. If we can find those who will take the time to get to know us, it is possible to cultivate a close peer relationship or two in school.

> I had a best friend from fourth to ninth grade (she moved out of state). All other friends have been transient. (Widders)

> I was bullied from the first day of school until the eighth grade. After that I made one friend. Many people find me interesting (at least at first) but I try to keep them away because I don't want people in my life. (Siv)

We don't cultivate or maintain "appropriate peer relationships." When we're younger we may be attracted to older people because of our intellectual maturity and hyperlexia, but as we get older, we may feel more comfortable with younger people because we don't mature emotionally. As adults we find people our own age boring and lacking in similar interests. For example, new sounds in the form of alternative music are incredibly important to me/us, but many people my age still listen to what they did when they were teenagers or else they have migrated over to country music the way old people migrate to Florida. They dress old-fashioned and wear their hair in styles they deem "suitable" for their age. To me they just seem staid. When I attend a rare dinner party, it is a short matter of time before all conversation starts to sound like the teacher from Charlie Brown ("wah wah, wah wah wah wah wah"). No matter how nice or intelligent everyone is, I just want to go home, put on my tutu and roller blade. I simply have great difficulty finding people who are open and youthful, yet mature and experienced in a way I relate to.

> I am a mother and yet my room looks like a child's room with a single bed, my teddy, my elephant collection, and little trinkets and things. I live like a kid. I also feel as if my emotions are both rudimentary and somewhat extreme. I am prone to tantrums and meltdowns. I feel out of my depth around adults unless it is special interest related. I am 47. I suppose I look my age, although I dress like a university student. (Camilla)

Ironically I like teenagers more now than I did when I was one. I've caught up in some ways—shop at the same stores they do, listen to the same bands, and like most of the same films. I am now, at first glance, *cool*. Yet after a few minutes of conversation, our intellectual and neurological differences become apparent on both sides. I find them unripe and preoccupied with hair. They find me shocking, strange and amusing…sometimes intimidating because of my bluntness. And in many ways they've passed me by again—I still want to watch children's movies and play games while they are enthused about boys and their future.

I find joy in computer games, in films like Harry Potter and Star Trek, and it seems that some people find me a bit childish because of this. I like to talk about it a lot as well. (Siv)

I don't *think* that I look, act and feel younger than I am, I *know* I do. I'm not irresponsible, just hyper and active like a younger person is. I have a lot of younger friends. I don't have any problems in particular with people my own age, save that I sometimes think they are boring. (Dame Kev)

As a person on the spectrum, I do have both compassion and empathy for many people, but that is not the same as friendship. There are people I like, those I admire, those whose company and conversation I enjoy in small doses, but I do not enjoy doing the things that women are supposed to enjoy doing with each other—shopping, movies, lunching, etc.

I am eccentric and well loved, I have a good sense of humor and am a good mimic. But I cannot feel connection with others in a manner that lasts over space and time. Many mistake my one-on-one "intensity" for some kind of special friendship "intimacy." I operate at a depth most people do not. (Camilla)

Because of our myriad sensory and social issues, many Aspergirls socialize only with their partners and children, because they understand us. We have control over what activities we will do with them. A friend who invites you to an event may not fully understand your reticence and concerns if they don't take the time to read and research AS.

There are times that I look at other people and wonder what its like to have friends but my husband is my best friend; we have an AS son and we all have a ton of fun together. (Nikki)

School and work gives us a pool from which, by odds, we might meet someone we connect with. But once we're out of school and especially if we're out of work, we can be quite isolated.

> I am a little lonely. It's always been hard for me to make friends and I have spent a lot of time inside the house the last few months, living at my parents'. At this stage, where academics stops structuring life for me and I have to structure it myself, it's been very difficult to work up the self-motivation to even leave my bedroom. (Stella)

> The only place I meet new people is at work. I don't have many friends, but I also don't actively try to make new friends. (Jen)

We have to get creative and seek out kindred spirits if we want friends. Special interests and group activities give us somewhere to go, *if* we can afford to go out at all (many of us spend our lives in financial straits). But we're still Aspies and may have a hard time taking that step to conversation.

> I have *no* friends! I have tried joining clubs, going to lessons, and all the usual palaver, and it doesn't work. Say it's a knitting class…at the end I've learned to knit, but I haven't met anyone or spoken to anyone much. If I *have* had a conversation, it was probably pretty forced. (Polly)

> I go to local film industry events and I see the same faces over and over again and get comfortable with some of them. This makes them acquaintances, though, not friends. My life isn't stable enough for *hanging out with the girls*-type friends—no money for one thing, plus too much stress to just hang and be casual. (Anemone)

Facebook, Twitter, and other internet tools can be extremely helpful in maintaining at least some semblance of a social life. They don't cost money, and since a large majority of us express ourselves better in writing than in conversation, it is possible to conduct fairly meaningful relationships online.

> I don't do well in person, but the internet has served me well. I can be the me that's stuck inside my head here…I am on one particular message board a lot. That's my home! I have lots of e-friends but locally I have no one. (Elfinia)

Online socializing avoids the group setting while, at the same time, gives us a feeling of being part of a community. Some find the growing sense of community among those with Asperger's means it is possible to have several friends that are also on the spectrum. It feels really good to talk to those who understand, to whom you do not constantly have to explain yourself. The other edge to the sword is that we may develop an "*us* and *them*" mentality.

> I long ago stopped trying to be close friends with non-spectrum people and only have friends I understand and who understand me. (Pokégran)

Younger Aspergirls have more need for "real world" friends, someone to sit with at lunch, play with after school, and share experiences with. This may impact our lives even more than our male counterparts—female friendships are based far more on social skills than male ones, which have more to do with shared activities or interests than conversation. The loneliness a young Aspergirl feels means that she might not be too discriminating.

> I would take whatever friends I could get. Often kids who didn't speak English. (Olive)

While it is true that some Aspergirls just don't want friends and are happy being alone, the thing I have found in my research is not so much an innate lack of desire for friends, but an acceptance of the fact they will never have them.

I only have a few acquaintances and one friend, really, who I don't see that often. Yes, I've given up for the most part. I don't know how to initiate or sustain friendship. If I call someone I think they will see me as weird/childish in mannerism. (Elle)

In lieu of human friendship, many Aspergirls allow only four-legged, furry, or feathered friends into their hearts. All but a few said that her pets were her closest companions.

Animals are people who are easier to get on with and befriend than humans. They are honest and accepting. Their needs and demands are simple, understandable, and easy to meet. They don't play mind games. (Pokégran)

As much as we feel alienated at times, we also alienate others. One of the ways we do this is by shutting out those who don't share our passions. I tried to get my teenage best friends to be as obsessed with Tolkien and music as I was but they bonded together in their hunt for more "normal" pursuits (i.e. jobs and boys), and I was left behind. I felt incredibly hurt, though I'd really left them no choice *but* to exclude me, since I made my contempt for their preferences obvious.

I tend to put people on a pedestal and then they fall off very quickly when I find they don't share one of my narrow interests even though they pretended to in the beginning. I feel betrayed by their lie. (Sam)

We have short-term memory issues so while we might be vehemently angry at someone for a while, we can quite literally forget why we were so mad after a time. This may cause us to go back again and again to the same unhealthy friendship or relationship, with the same patterns of behavior and expectations, until something quite dramatic happens—enough to lose empathy completely and close a door forever.

Doctors and the diagnostic manuals are telling us that we are not cultivating "appropriate peer relationships" but in light of all these things it makes sense. We seem, feel and act younger than our age but it is not appropriate for us to "hang out" with teens or children. Other people our age bore us or we can't relate to them. We have a tendency to stay at home. Once we're of post-education age, and especially if we're out of work or in the wrong job, it means our options will be decreased and limited, and that it will be difficult to have a large or typical number of friends.

Some of us are okay with that.

> I was always unable to connect but didn't feel lonely.
> (Kiley)

ADVICE TO ASPERGIRLS

If you have confidence in yourself, that confidence spills over into your social skills and into the social arena. People sense when you know your worth and they respond to it. It helps to be validated but even before validation comes belief in self and in one's own thoughts and abilities.

> I am a Lord of the Rings lovin', Renaissance Faire going, comic book reading, typical geek. Probably before I was even five I knew I'd never fit in; knew I was different and just decided "to heck with it" and embraced my geekiness. Being a nerd is one of the things I really love about myself. (Elfinia)

If you are truly happy alone, then you are lucky, for it is peaceful and you definitely have more time to engage in your passions, whether they be writing books or painting pictures or just hanging out watching British period films and kung fu flicks. But, I want you to please take some time to ask yourself if you are truly happy, or if, like many, you've simply given up. I've been there. Until very recently I'd become resigned to a life alone, where I'd eventually die alone and my body would lay partially eaten by rabid squirrels until some pesky Jehovah's Witness came to my door and saw it through the window.

But then an old friend came back into my life, regaling me with tales of food and fun and people and drink and music and dance and it made me angry that I'd let life get me so down that I basically laid down and said "I quit!" I was using work as a shield, keeping myself cruelly busy and then every night I'd sit alone, watching movies, pretending that I'd had a full enough life; that this was okay.

I disclosed Asperger's to this old friend and asked if I would be given acceptance and leeway for sometimes unorthodox behavior. To my delight, this friend has now read up on AS, asks thought-provoking questions and tells everyone about this great gal he knows that has Asperger's. He in turn, shares what he has learned with others and is educating the world in his own small way. He has accepted me completely although he does challenge my boundaries. He is now my partner. Other friends have not been so understanding, but that is no reason to give up.

If you want more friends, *do something about it.* Don't give up. Use your interests and strengths and visualization skills to figure out how to go about it. It's important to understand that you can still be friends with people who don't passionately share all your interests. This is how we broaden our horizons. You may also have to leave your room, unless you are okay with cyber friendships only. They may not strengthen your face-to-face skills but they are a good place to start and you can develop some rapport with people in this way. Safety first—don't give out addresses, real names, etc., to people you meet online. In addition to chat rooms and forums, there are software programs which enable you to video-chat with friends for free as long as you both have a camera. You get much more of a sense of a person if you can see them while speaking. I find this to be true—for although eye contact can be difficult I find it hard to discern a person's intentions from their voice, and find reassurance in faces…and *kind* eyes. Again, follow safety rules.

Another thing about the internet is that because people can and do say whatever comes to mind, it is not a full picture of someone. People can take on other personas and mislead you. I frequently find a phenomenon called "internet balls" on forums, where people say things that they probably wouldn't say in person. Be yourself and be tactful—if you do eventually want to meet someone you've met online, you want to have given them a glimpse of the real you, a complete picture, just as you would want from them.

Don't throw a friend away because you don't like or agree with 10 percent of their behavior and don't give people a small window of time to perform to your expectations. There is no human piece of perfection that will meet all our criteria. We have control issues and we need to know what to expect, but give yourself and your friends a little room to maneuver and to mess up without judging too harshly. For we do judge, don't we?—both ourselves and others.

As far as maturity goes, as long as you are addressing your needs and the needs of those who depend on you, especially children, then carry on wearing those Wonder Woman pajamas.

ADVICE TO PARENTS

Like the parents in Roald Dahl's *Matilda*, there are some who don't understand their daughter's bookish ways and solitary nature. They might think that if they push their daughter out of doors and into the waiting arms of other kids (who often have fists and throwable objects at the end of them) that the girl will benefit more from that. There is a time and a place for socializing but she's better off seeking out like-minded kids rather than defaulting to whomever is available in her neighborhood.

Young people with AS have told me that social skills training has really helped them. Explore the options in your area, through your local autism services, school, and therapists. There are also books on body language, etc.

Find clubs or activities she'll enjoy, for example if she's a science geek, find out if there are clubs or activities at her local science museum. Pursuing intellectual things that make her happy will bring her into contact with kindred spirits and like-minded souls and then socializing will come almost naturally.

Some parents take away internet privileges from their AS child thinking that will get them out into the world. I don't recommend that…the internet is our favorite link to people, organizations, and information, and "real world connections" can be made from it. There are lots of ways to make a living online as well and you must work with your Aspergirl's strengths, not against them.

If your daughter is unhappy and doesn't have enough friends, you and other family members can take an active role. If you know someone your daughter might get along with, it couldn't hurt to arrange a meeting. You have to trust your own instincts, as long as it's someone she'd like and not someone you'd like her to like.

> I meet friends through my husband or through other family members or long time friends. Often, those are the friendships that last longer. It may be an odd thing to say, but it is like the people who know me well screen the person to see if we might get along. (Dame Kev)

One mother, Deborah, started an AS support group to give her and her daughter a chance to meet others with AS in their area. That's what I call being proactive! Maybe you already have a local group you could attend. Give it a chance, you have nothing to lose and everything to gain.

10

HIGHER LEARNING

College/university is a whole different ball game than high school and grade school. The classes are partly of our own choosing, they are more challenging, we have more autonomy, and barring any law-breaking activities, no one really cares what you do as long as you get your work in on time. At first it is heaven, and we may thrive, but soon, the usual challenges of Asperger's start to pop their heads up. *Remember us?* They'll ask. *You thought you got rid of us, but we're still here!*

Leaving home, maintaining independence, working a part-time job and managing to get to classes on time and hand in assignments are difficult enough for any young adult, but with AS it can be overwhelming.

Socializing is difficult and you may not see a single familiar face (on the other hand, this can be a relief); dorm life messes with all our privacy and sensory issues and we may suffer from lack of sleep, keeping track of deadlines and managing large assignments simultaneously, etc. These are some of the challenges we face. Some of us will have a hard time staying motivated and will feel that we are in over our heads. Others will float like ducks on water, *because* of AS—focus, need for routines, and learning, learning, learning!

I excelled in academia! Grade and high school are full of dumb rules and egos, and you have to endure it all day long. At university, you do the work or not, you go to class when you need to—and that's that. (Widders)

An Aspergirl's experience at college will vary depending on how high-functioning she is, her particular challenges, and the school she attends.

As of September I'm a PhD student. I failed out of my first two years of college. I was at a huge public school in 600 person lectures, and I just couldn't do it. After switching to a smaller school I did very well. It's taken me some extra time, but it was worth it... I now have plenty of support. (Andi)

Because we have a strong thirst for knowledge, and a chameleon nature, our areas of interest can change rapidly and dramatically, causing confusion about what to study. Some may change course a few times, but I believe that we will usually default back into whatever our earliest interests were. Many of us will know at an early age what we want to be when we grow up. If we pursue that with our legendary diligence and don't get sidetracked, we have a good chance for success. Knowing yourself and what you need before you go will optimize your experience. In *Asperger's on the Job* (Simone 2010), I talk about identifying any triggers in your potential career—things that push your autistic buttons that might detract from your pleasure, enthusiasm, and ability to cope. There will always be triggers, but if you work within your areas of greatest natural passion you will have a better chance of seeing your degree through.

I'm studying interactive system design. I can't imagine doing anything else. (Andi)

Many of us will become interested in psychology and the helping professions along the way, either because of our diagnosis or in search of it. We find we want to nurture and help others in their journeys because we know how hard it can be.

> I am currently an undergrad student majoring in psychology. I initially started as pre-vet, but then suddenly my interest in biology dropped, and I became intensely focused on psychology. My diagnosis had a huge effect on this. (Shannon)

> I went to the Royal Northern College of Music as a composer but I learned after being in hospital that I actually wanted to be a nurse. I am two years into a three-year qualification now. (Kylli)

Because of a combination of high intelligence, low self-esteem and eagerness to begin our new careers, we sometimes bite off more than we can chew. One of the key things to realize about female AS is this: Society expects us to handle things well based on our intelligence and appearance of normality. Unfortunately, we often demand the same of ourselves. Even if we can handle it academically or intellectually, it doesn't mean we can handle it physically or emotionally. We need extra time, extra patience, and more sensitivity than most people. Full stop.

> I majored in both Journalism and English Lit. I overloaded on all of my classes, because I felt that I needed to. Part of those classes included work preparation and study. Despite taking twice as many classes as most other students took those two years, my grades were still high. Eventually, I was forced to quit school due to academic probation and angering a dean with a practical joke. (Dame Kev)

> I was dux of my high school senior year. I attempted college three times. Ended up in psychiatric unit. Could

not cope with people or organization requirements. Dropped out. (Camilla)

Offices of Disability Services (ODS): There is a lack of understanding in some university ODS of what Asperger's and autism really are. Some have a working knowledge of Asperger's, while others know little of the syndrome, citing a lack of funds for specialized training. When I called a few to ask questions, and told them I had Asperger's, some spoke to me in a slow voice, like I was mentally challenged.

The amount of help you get might depend on something as arbitrary as whether or not the disability staff-person has an Autistic or Aspergian in their family, giving them a personal glimpse. For those who have not lived it, encountered it firsthand, do not know what it entails unless they've made it a special subject of study.

AS is in some respects a disability—no one is allowed to tell a person in a wheelchair that if they want to get to the second floor, they must climb the stairs. But when we try to explain our problems, such as auditory processing difficulties, or social interactions, the response from staff and counselors is usually to tell us that we must "try to get on with it" and "try to get along with people." Of course we must, but we're not told *how* in a way that we can actually manage. And unfortunately we find that other people don't always try to get along with us. Still, you *should* try to get some amenities for having AS—longer deadlines, more time on tests, and counseling from someone who really knows the syndrome.

I lived in the dorms and it was hell without a pet; I now have an emotional support dog that I can have in no pets housing. (Shannon)

I get to use a laptop in all my classes. I get outlines of things from the instructor when available so I can be sure to focus on the important details. I can also get help explaining from disability services, how my AS may cause problems. (Ata)

Graduate school has been an ongoing struggle for me. When I presented my disability and the diagnosis information from my doctor and therapist to the woman who handles the disabilities accommodations she was far from accommodating. She said that they had a problem meeting my needs. Academics is not an issue, it's the social interaction that drives me crazy. And our education system is not yet understanding of this problem for those on the spectrum; especially adults. (Brandi)

Sensory, social and cognitive processing issues may mean that we may have to find our own way of doing things and in our own time.

Took me five years to complete a three-year degree. I couldn't absorb auditory lectures. Now I'm doing an online MBA and getting top marks. (Kes)

Our experiences as always will be helped or hindered by those that enter and inhabit our lives. Most of those who have a postgraduate degree finished by their own perseverance, not always with the support and cooperation of others.

I was accepted into a Communication Sciences program (MS). Once they realized I had a disability most of the faculty cold-shouldered me. One asked me to leave. I now have a master of science degree. (Widders)

I have a bachelors and masters in astrophysics. I struggled immensely with severe anxiety disorders; terrible treatment by professors; I was often mute and I underachieved. I am now writing up my PhD. (Michelle)

I completed a bachelors degree. I nearly died getting it. If I had known when I began about AS, I would have had a support network in place which would have saved a lot of suffering. (Heather)

I was lucky in that I had supportive staff and friends—they are all a godsend. (Stella)

One thing I encountered while studying counseling and psychology was a lack of imagination and mental rigidity in my teachers (and no, they were not AS—at least not that I know of). Because of Asperger/fluid intelligence, I was able to make some unique connections that was beyond what I was being taught, and I was misunderstood. I also had ethical objections to certain aspects of psychology. I believe that because of emotional innocence, the most idealistic of us might find we become disillusioned when we discover real world applications of our areas of passion.

I obtained my BS in Environmental Advocacy but I did not work in the field for long because the people I encountered frustrated me in their lack of open-mindedness and seeming lack of spirituality. (Ann Marie)

I have spent the last six years as a school-based speech language pathologist. I hated working in schools. The admin and faculty tend to be very disability-intolerant. They also tend to talk horribly about parents behind their backs. Of course there are good people, but not enough. I am now doing home-based services. I like it much better. (Widders)

Many Aspies love math, because in those classes it doesn't matter what the instructor thinks of you, only whether you get the answer right. I found the subjectivity of grading in essay or presentation-based classes (based on the good opinion of my teachers) very frustrating. If I had to do it again, I would have switched schools to find teachers I connected with instead of dropping out. Looking for reasons to leave, burning bridges, and quitting before we fail is an Asperger specialty, one that we need to watch out for. Essentially I used all of these things, along with bullying, as an excuse to quit.

> I eventually finished my HND (Higher National Diploma (UK)) but could not manage a degree. I have far fewer qualifications than I should have. I have never been able to sort that out. (Sam)

ADVICE TO ASPERGIRLS

When it comes to college, I would say to all Aspergirls *please* don't give up. There is so much at stake—money, time, future quality of life, independence. The girls I interviewed have achieved much and it would be tragic to see any of them give up before they reach their goals.

Don't bite off more than you can chew and take five classes when you should only be taking one. Your intellect may be able to handle it, but your emotions and senses might not. Instead of filling your free time with more classes, use it to decompress, stabilize, and take care of your physical and emotional health.

It is important to recruit as much help as you can. Start with the Office of Disability Services, find out what they know and how accommodating they really are. If they are not as progressive as you'd like, and you need assistance teaching them about AS, there may be some advocates out there who don't charge an arm and a leg, or perhaps someone at your local autism services might be able to lend a hand. Even partners or parents could make contact with the ODS, for self-advocacy is very difficult. I would suggest you write a list of what you need to succeed in your courses. Read it a few times, make sure it's streamlined and do-able (you don't want to ask for too much or for the impossible) and then give it to your teachers and ODS staff. Then follow up. Sometimes we have to be stronger than we think we can be. I know how hard it is. *Keep your eye on the prize, and be willing to compromise.* The autistic community is a subculture, one that the nonautistic world is just becoming familiar with. We are pioneers and the choices we make can have a positive impact on those who come after.

Figure out your bliss and then find the most practical education and qualifications you can to pursue it. We do tend to change course—look at the big picture as thoroughly as you can. Visualize the life you want and use that logical mind of yours to get there. If you do not yet know what you want to do, choose a degree that has flexible outcomes and career prospects, working with your strengths.

Most of us are self-taught and see no reason to stop that trend. Some of us might even find college a bit slow, or some of the classes we must take too far outside our areas of interest. You must have that piece of paper to prove to others your worth, and to even get a shoe in the door for most positions. Not finishing university will profoundly impact your income. Seek support, disclose your needs if not your condition, report bullies, keep your head up (not down) and stick with it.

It's possible that some of your teachers may only be there to have access to facilities and research grants. If you feel that their heart isn't in teaching, switch if and when you can, but you're always going to encounter people whose motives are a bit mixed, who are less than enthusiastic for their job. Don't let another's apathy infect you.

Plan on taking a little longer than most to finish your degree (if necessary) and don't beat yourself up for social or learning difficulties. While we have an average to above-average IQ, we still have some cognitive quirks that can make certain types of learning difficult for us. For example, we may do better with written or visual learning and retain nothing from auditory lectures. If you are struggling with a course get extra tutoring and find a way of learning that will stick in your mind. Try recording lectures and then typing, writing or even drawing them up afterward to fix into your long-term memory.

If your college counselor says that your problems have more to do with depression or some other psychological condition than Asperger's, change counselors! Find someone who understands and will take into account the pervasive underlying nature of AS. If your counselor is willing to read this book and others on Asperger's, particularly female Asperger's, then give him or her a chance, for you are doing your part to educate another human being on the topic. They may then help others like you in the future. Never underestimate how many people you can educate and how many others they can, in turn, help.

There are special university programs for people on the spectrum (such as *Pathway* at UCLA's extension). My feeling is that these are for people who have great difficulty with life skills as they tend to be both expensive and residential. There may be more appearing every year so research if you are thinking of going back.

ADVICE TO PARENTS

Make sure your daughter is in contact with the Disability Office. Find someone there you can connect with and to whom you can impart literature and understanding of the syndrome. Many of the people in these offices are young and inexperienced but have good intentions, and if you approach them as such, they will be more willing to listen to what you say. Before you educate them, their knowledge of AS may be limited to "social awkwardness and a literal mind." They probably have no idea of the complex nature of Asperger's and the many positives.

Encourage your daughter, talk to her about school, find out if she is receiving the time and attention she needs and do give her an understanding ear when she needs it. But she needs more than an ear. Sometimes she needs an advocate for she may not be able to advocate for herself.

CHAPTER *11*

EMPLOYMENT AND CAREER

There are various pitfalls and challenges in the workplace specific to those with Asperger syndrome. Not least of all is getting a job in the first place. There is no magic bullet, but there are several dozens, if not hundreds, of techniques, strategies, and points to know about AS and work. The main problem for most of us is that we have a hard time holding onto jobs for social reasons. I cannot stress enough how important it is to work with your strengths and acknowledge your triggers—things that push your autistic buttons—so that you choose the right career path. (To that end I created the Personal Job Map which can be found in *Asperger's on the Job* (Simone 2010).) The areas we want to work in run the gamut from painting, drawing, design, music composition and performance, writing, architecture, engineering, physics, to medicine. Nobody I have ever interviewed said it was their lifelong aspiration to be a secretary, sales girl, or waitress, but that is often the type of position we find ourselves in, especially if we do not get a degree. Those jobs don't require degrees, but they *do* require people skills—*the thing we lack the most*. If a person with AS can work in the field of their passion, their obsession, their "zone activity," they will be much more apt to want to go to work and be much more fulfilled as a person.

Financial stability is important to everyone, male, female, AS or NT; however, I think it is in some ways most crucial for an Aspergirl. Many Aspergirls remain single out of choice, limiting household financial income. She is also left without "male protection"—you know, the physical presence that keeps mechanics and plumbers from taking advantage. She will be at the mercy and whim of others if she cannot stand on her own two feet. If you have money, you can buy and/or live in the kind of environment which is crucial to your sensory issues—i.e. a quiet house as opposed to a cheap and noisy apartment building. You can pay for yourself to go places and not have to rely on a partner. Feeling powerless and ineffectual is a huge part of female AS and poverty will only increase that feeling.

Aspergirls often know when they're quite young what they want to do and with the right support they may achieve it. They are more likely to have a satisfying career if they can stick out their degree.

> I always wanted to be a librarian. I am a specialist in cataloging and have worked as a librarian for 20 years. Today I work with a wide range of material, from medieval manuscripts to eighteenth-century collections. Time and place cease to exist, when I'm working with my collections. (Siv)

> I work in the media, and it was my first choice. I'm an autistic person who communicates for a living, and relishes the irony! I got a job with my current employer straight out of uni and I've stuck with them ever since. I'm very, very grateful, because the organization I'm with has quite a high population of Aspies (whether they know it or not!) and is very tolerant of eccentricity. (Polly)

For those whose aspirations are of an artistic or musical nature, it is very hard to make a living at those things, but it is not impossible. One of the pitfalls of this kind of career is often the lack of financial stability. You may also feel that you have not been given your just deserts; that your music or art is not being recognized for its worth. There is an awful lot of subjectivity in artistic careers and often our progress may be impeded by poor social skills, which may frustrate us. The other thing about these types of careers is that you have to do something else for money until you get established. Most of us won't want to go to college full time and get a time-consuming career in something else when we just want to paint or sing for a living, so we will start in those dead end jobs such as waitressing that require people skills and possibly end up in them as well. That means obscurity, poverty and very high stress levels for most of us.

> I write in the hopes of writing something that will sell, including a major research project on the evolution of culture. I have been on welfare for close to 12 years of my adult life. (Anemone)

> My first choice from age five or so was to be an artist. I'm now a successful artist in Australia, also a speaker on ASD (autistic spectrum disorder) issues. I work in isolation and live reclusively but successfully. I sell my work, represented by commercial galleries and have won awards. However, over the years I had many menial jobs for periods of time. I usually left jobs after a year or so because I could not cope. (Camilla)

I went to college for music but was soon singing professionally so I dropped out. When my band broke up, I became a waitress, secretary, receptionist, hostess, babysitter, housewife, and telemarketer and just about everything else that could possibly mess with my sensory and social issues. The list is much longer than I care to recall. Never again did I reach the heights of success as a singer as I did at the age of 18 to 19. It took 20 more years of struggle before I finally gave up. All the while, I burned through a string of countless meaningless jobs that did nothing for my self-esteem, that did not utilize my gifts, and that wreaked havoc with my Asperger's, or else my AS wreaked havoc with them. And although I've found success in the last few years as a writer and consultant, if I had to do it over again I would have finished my degree and avoided the menial jobs. It sometimes takes a hard lesson to get us back on track.

> I am not currently employed. I have had over 30 jobs. Fast food worker, dishwasher, nanny, PCA (personal care assistant), mental health worker, behavioral technician in an inpatient psych unit, production worker, sanitation worker, press operator, bartender, retail associate, housing support specialist, caretaker/housekeeper, nursing assistant, program assistant, and teacher's aide. These are all I can remember. I'm now a graduate student. (Brandi)

Getting a degree is a crucial part of success for most of us, as is working with our strengths. But it is no guarantee. We must also work on our deficits or we will have a hard time securing a satisfying position.

> I *hate* cleaning. It's so mindless. And what a cruddy end for a person with a university degree: Custodian? House cleaner? Gads, the shame! I am not currently employed. I have not been successful at maintaining a job for more than four months. (Heather)

As I state in my employment book, most Aspies want to go to work, do their job and go home, but it's not that simple. People set the tone of our experience. That is why many Aspergirls try to circumvent working with others, by working from home, or with animals:

> I don't work. I stay home and home-school my son. I just can't deal with people for long hours. (Nikki)

> I love being a groomer. I feel an affinity with my dog and the ones I groom as well. I feel like I'm a part of their world, like a mother wolf. (Elfinia)

I've talked a lot about intellectual challenge and fulfillment, but of course not every Aspergirl is a creative genius. Some like simple and repetitive work.

> At the age of 13 I decided to be a dental hygienist. I love the repetitive work of removing deposits from teeth. The hard part is working with the people attached to the teeth and all of the personality issues that arise. (Jen)

Aspies can burn very hot and cold on hobbies and vocations, so it is good to stay in the area of your passion so that it will hold your attention and focus for a long time, and you will be paid to be "in the zone." If you do not find work in one of your areas of obsession, you will probably be distracted, bored, depressed; you may even find you become physically sick. We need our obsessions. They give our psyches an anchor, they give our thoughts ritual and routine which we know is extremely important. Without them, our thoughts will just float about in the breeze like a stray balloon, not going anywhere, never really getting lift-off.

> I get so stressed being with people all day and not being able to pursue my interests. I stay up until the wee hours feeding my interests and get little sleep. (Widders)

Temple Grandin says to people on the spectrum "sell your work not yourself" and she is right—but how do you do that in a culture where personality sells, and the psychometric or *personality test* is often a required step toward getting a job? The so-called personality test exposes our social and cognitive differences (not necessarily deficits) and could cause a person with Asperger's to lose a job before they get it, before they have a chance to show what they're made of. Career satisfaction, and lowering the number of people with autism who are out of work or underemployed, comes down to recognition of our talents, acceptance of our deficits, and utilization of our strengths.

It doesn't matter anymore that you are a dedicated, hard worker with a good work ethic. They would rather have someone talkative and outgoing. I've never held a job longer than a year. Currently I am unemployed and because of the economy I will have to take any job that I can get whether it is appropriate for my personality or not. (Elle)

I know this question is meant for adults, but I'll answer anyway. I do worry about getting a job… I don't know how I'll handle the interviews. I have a very hard time looking people in the eye, especially strangers. (Megan)

Underemployed and overqualified most of life. Worst aspect about AS. (Michelle)

Disclosure—when and where to do it, if at all—always comes down to a cross between personal choice and necessity. Partial disclosure is another option—asking for individual accommodations rather than disclosing the fact you have AS. Some of us see it as our duty to disclose, to spread awareness of what AS means. But disclosure, even full disclosure which incorporates discussion and literature, is no guarantee of accommodation or true understanding. That's why many of us opt for self-employment as artists, writers, lawyers, etc., or work in Aspie-friendly fields such as engineering and software developing, where our quirks will hardly be noticed.

Getting the right education in your field, making good choices and not giving up on being a useful part of society is so important, especially for naïve Aspergirls. If we don't make things happen *for* us, things tend to happen *to* us…

I've been working at renaissance festivals and living in a tent or my car. Used to traveling to a new show every two months with other social outcasts. Two years ago I was in a bad car accident (rear ended while waiting to make a left turn in a 70 mph zone) That left me with 11 herniated discs, fibromyalgia, and no car. I found myself stuck in bed in a little shack. I've been floating (homeless) for five or so years now. (Bramble)

As I stated in the Introduction, I actually think that problems with employment and the economy are why more people are being diagnosed. The high cost of living, having to work longer, harder and having more competition to get jobs as well as hurdles like the personality test mean that we are smacked in the face with the realization that we are not coping as well as we should be and we want to find out why.

ADVICE TO ASPERGIRLS

It is possible for an Aspergirl to have a thoroughly satisfying career. You must work within one of your areas of passion, get through your degree or training as best you can (hopefully with enough help) and then find a position with at least some autonomy, prestige and enough intellectual challenge. At the same time, you must respect your sensory needs.

To a large extent it is true that social skills count more than actual work ethic in many jobs. There is social skills training, in the form of books, groups, therapy, etc.

There are jobs you can do alone, with little social contact, and there is also the option of self-employment. Business owners and the self-employed often struggle but there is both peace and satisfaction in doing what you want and being your own boss. But self-employment can have its own set of difficulties, including financial instability, multiple and varied responsibilities (e.g. even if you're an artist you may also have to be your own secretary, marketing person and accountant) and too little social contact to help you grow that aspect of yourself.

Those who are stay-at-home moms, too, seem happy and fulfilled. However, to hope for and rely upon the thought that a man will support you is just not practical. Most men these days can't afford to support a woman even if they wanted to. An Aspergirl must face the world with the aim of supporting herself, being fulfilled and not needing anyone else to support her—especially in the United States, where benefits are very hard to come by and have several hurdles, all of which seem to have the aim of humiliating you and eroding self-esteem.

If you have an inclination toward the arts, I do not want to discourage you, but take it from one who has been there—you must get qualifications and have two or three back-up plans that are virtually as appealing as your main goal. Follow your bliss, get as much education as you can, and have two or three "Plan Bs." This is *not* a cop-out, this is called being smart, for just because you don't have a safety net, doesn't mean you won't need one.

Not every Aspergirl is a creative genius. You might find that the routine and predictability of being an accountant provides the surety and tranquility you require. And not everyone hates being a cashier—some with high-functioning autism (HFA) and AS like the scripted life of the checkout counter.

Work is an interruption into our routine—but new routines can be made. Meal planning, sleep aids, and constructive use of time spent out of work will ease the transition.

Take the time to get to know yourself and really be honest about what you want and what you can handle. If you are going to work with a job coach, make sure they have an in-depth understanding of AS. You and/or they can read my book on employment (Simone 2010) to get a thorough understanding of the many social, emotional and environmental issues at play. There are others too: Roger N. Meyer's *Asperger Syndrome Employment Workbook* (2001) and Sarah Hendrickx's *Asperger Syndrome and Employment* (2009) are both excellent.

Make financial stability and independence your passion and seek it with the same legendary focus and diligence with which you do almost everything.

ADVICE TO PARENTS

Do encourage your Aspergirl to get the highest qualifications she can in her field of interest, as well as social skills training and whatever other practical applications she needs help with. As we discussed in the previous chapter, education is fraught with several difficulties in itself, but it must be navigated if your daughter is going to fulfill her potential. An Aspergirl's happiness depends on a combination of meaningful work, limited friction, freedom to create, and lots of control. On the other hand don't push too much—our passions change and just because we are fascinated with space doesn't mean we want to be an astronaut. Aspergirls need to find work that works with their AS traits but doesn't push their autistic buttons.

Many Aspergirls will be frightened of work. She will try her hand at a job and find that she is not fitting in; she may get bullied or just feel really uncomfortable. It is frustrating for parents when their 18-year-old is still living at home (or their 38-year old) and they just can't seem to find a job that works. It is not that your daughter is lazy—it is so difficult to explain to someone who has not lived through it, but feeling like a black sheep, feeling awkward, uncomfortable, scrutinized, having our rituals and routines interrupted, not having control over our environment, all these things make finding a job we like incredibly difficult. Your patience will likely be tested. The usual milestones will probably happen, just not as quickly as you might hope or expect. Do your best not to be angry at your daughter for finding it hard fitting into the world of work, but be supportive and discuss with her what her dreams are, and what the possibilities for making them happen involve.

CHAPTER 12

MARRIAGE AND COHABITATION

For an Aspergirl, home is sacrosanct. Men may have their caves but so do we, and ours are generally much more comfortable to live in. Home is where we have complete control, over sights, sounds, smells, temperature, and textures. Where we can truly be ourselves. If we have enough money to live in our choice environment, home is heaven on earth. Why on earth would we want to mess with that?

> The idea of living with someone scares me senseless. I've done it before for five years, and I shut down to cope with it. I don't want to give up myself again. I hope to find someone who is happy just to continue "as is" without expectations. (Kes)

I've spoken to Aspergirls who are happily single, who don't want anything in the house hairier than their guinea pig. Others want to find a boyfriend who they can see occasionally while they keep on living alone. Others are married or living with someone and are very happy. Marriage is another situation about which we all have different viewpoints and experiences.

The pluses of living with someone is having someone to share bills with; someone to impress when you've created something brilliant, someone to laugh with when you watch something funny, and someone to talk to besides yourself; a steady supply of sex and someone to go on outings with. It means someone to keep us from falling completely into our solitary habits and routines without any deviation whatsoever—living alone doesn't pull us out of ourselves or challenge us to grow in any way.

> I'm a bit lonely. I have some friends but not a relationship. I often long for affection and comfort and stability. Living alone is bad for me, I'm best with someone to drag me out of the house. (Andi)

Marriage is difficult; it is a series of exchanges, compromises, and conversations. It means sharing your physical space, meals, having less alone time. It may mean taking on his kids, his dog, his friends, his smells and his messes—and vice versa. For the *non*autistic woman, it is often difficult enough to find the right man. For *us*, it really takes a special kind of person to be in it for the long haul.

> I need my partner to keep me sane! He knows more about AS than me and he's very aware about how to handle my meltdowns or upsets. (Sarah)

Self-awareness is truly knowing who you are, what you like, and what you don't. In our case it is also knowing to what extent your AS will affect you in a relationship. Not having a strong sense of identity and self-ness means that it might take us a bit longer to be ready for marriage than nonautistic girls. While some Aspergirls have known their partner since childhood and are quite happy, others married poorly pre-diagnosis. A successful marriage will depend upon that self-awareness and whether or not you have a partner who will educate himself, and work with Asperger's, not against it.

> I chose my Aspie husband because he was uncomplicated, straightforward, honest, and strong in areas that I am

weak. We connected on a non-verbal level. I knew he understood me and I understood him. (Jen)

Because we don't like the whole dating process, and because there may have been few men whom we had a romantic connection to, some of us jump very quickly into marriage. Aspergirls like myself have married because we were at a certain age; we didn't know what love was, we just thought it was the right time.

> I married twice, both times quickly without dating, and at the insistence of the other. I would not recommend this; both men ended up abusive. Now I love my solitude! (Widders)

We may also marry or cohabitate because we sense that we need someone to take care of us, or cover the bases we cannot, especially if we have problems with getting or keeping a job.

> I live with my boyfriend who is my carer. Only person I've liked living with. I don't think I'm in love. I feel love for someone else I can't have. (Michelle)

We are innocents. We believe what people tell us and we believe in keeping one's word. If someone says they love us and want to marry us, we generally assume they mean it even if their behavior contradicts their proclamation. I have been married twice. I do not like to be lonely, particularly when there is someone else in the room. I was very lonely with both my husbands. The first one was older and I thought he'd take care of me. He completely did not understand or like anything about me and left me with our daughter after about 18 months. The second person I married was 12 years younger than me. He, too, had nothing but criticisms and didn't seem to like or respect me. He also left, quite abruptly, and I never saw him again.

It's really important that a person with Asperger's is not criticized. That only makes us curl up into a ball. We need positive reinforcement for the good things we do, and then we will strive to do more of that. It takes a very special partner to understand this.

Many of the married Aspergirls I interviewed have diagnosed or suspected AS husbands. Whether or not your man is an Aspie, he needs to have some similar views as you on certain areas of life. If he is the kind of person who really cares about appearances and social conventions rather than integrity and depth; if he cares more about conformity than self-expression, or confidence than quality, you will have a hard time together. If he wants a wife who is going to be a social butterfly, multi-task, and be a soccer mom, he's going to be let down. He needs to understand that there is a big difference between not wanting to do something and not being able to do something.

> My Aspie husband is very understanding. We've been married for 30 years. We understand each other's need for space away from others at times. (Pokégran)

> I am happily married to a man with Asperger's. We met on a forum for adults with AS. He is older than I by a number of years and he grew up in an era when it was considered normal for the wife to stay at home and manage the household, so my joblessness doesn't bother him. We own a little house and live modestly on a budget. We try to be very patient and tolerant of one another's idiosyncrasies and quirks. Both of us were alone long enough to make us *very* grateful for our marriage. Years of loneliness and isolation taught both of us that no problem or issue in a marriage merits making a big deal of it, particularly to the point of damaging the relationship. (Heather)

It is no guarantee that just because your partner has AS you will automatically be perfect for each other. Two people who lack theory of mind, who are not truly in love, who are socially withdrawn and have sensory issues and meltdowns can mean drama and loneliness for both.

> I'm unhappy due to constant arguments in marriage. We can't seem to understand each other. He also does not seem to like sex as much as me and can't tell when I want it. (Sam)

Once we get to know ourselves and are no longer trying to be something we're not, we have a strange mix of values. Some of us can be very traditional and simple while others opt for an alternative lifestyle that suits their needs. But whichever we are, we are marching to our own drum; it's a decision that is coming from within.

> I think Mom should be home with the kids, while Dad works. I have a whole little spiel about how this would fix what's wrong with the world, but my views aren't always popular, especially in women's studies class. (Nikki)

> I have my main partner who I live with and a second boyfriend I see every Tuesday. Having two partners has worked out pretty well. Both my partners get along. It works out because the second boyfriend is very rigid and needs a lot of space. He would be nearly impossible to live with. (Olive)

> My son's father and I live in the same house, are friends, but live separate lives largely due to my autism spectrum disorder (ASD). We live fairly happily, however. (Camilla)

Some of us, because of the social criticisms and isolation we have had to endure, may have internalized that we don't "deserve" a truly wonderful partner; that being lonely might be the price we pay for being flawed. The right partner will look at those same attributes with a very different perspective than the wrong one.

I get very protective of her because she's my everything. I don't care about her quirks. That's not who she is, it's just a part of what makes her personality interesting. She's smart, funny, and honestly the bravest woman I've ever met. She's been through hell and came out ok. I'm sure some came from people not understanding her AS, but I don't care. She's mine, and I wouldn't change her. Well, I wish life had been a little easier for her, but she might have been different if it had been. (Dame Kev's husband)

Meltdowns and depressions can take on mammoth proportions for an Aspergirl and it takes a special man not to run away in the face of our emotional storms.

During the really terrible depressions my husband's vows of "in sickness and in health" truly shine through. As I lie in an almost catatonic state, he brings me food and juice even though he knows I will not eat; changes my pajamas and encourages me to shower. Sometimes I will open my eyes to find him lying next to me waiting for me to wake after many hours of sleep. He wipes my tears one-by-one offering comforting words which, although they never seem to rid me of depression, I believe they have been my sanity and without them I would not be here today. Sometimes he cries with me as though he can feel my pain but then I realize that this is not the case, he just misses me, he misses being an *us*, and this makes me cry more. Day after day, night after night, he waits for me. This is caretaking at its finest. (Brandi)

ADVICE TO ASPERGIRLS

I first chose potential mates based on physical attraction and mutual obsession. But a person married to an Aspergirl has to be nurturing, patient, and he has to read—for if he doesn't read about AS, he'll never get you. He has to be willing to compromise on noise levels, and everything from the fabrics of your furniture to where you live. He is going to have to be understanding and forgiving, for meltdowns, according to my research, happen to 97 percent of us at least now and then, and for some, they are quite frequent. There are myriad issues that will be affected by your AS and he is going to have to be able to live with that.

Likewise, you will have to compromise. He can't always be the caretaker and the one who gives in. You will have to force yourself out of your comfort zone for him whenever possible.

If you want a husband or partner and at times feel like you don't deserve one, I want you to remember what Dame Kev's husband said about her, and understand that you have the same right to be loved. No matter what your parents, siblings, even your children (for they can be our worst critics) and acquaintances say, you do deserve love and you shall have it if you believe it.

For those who are alone and happy, just check every now and then to make sure you *are* happy and not just resigned. Is it true happiness, or just the lesser of two evils? Just because you haven't met the right one yet, he or she may still be out there. Do know that someday you may decide life's a little richer when you have someone to share it with. Keep a little window of opportunity open even if you do not actively seek a mate.

Some Aspergirls have been so hurt and disappointed by marriage they have given up. They think cohabitation equals pain and stress. But once you have someone who is right for you, you'll be surprised at how different living with someone can be, how much more you can thrive. Emotional support and unconditional love are elusive but incredible things if you can find them and they can turn the darkest, loneliest life into something completely different. My favorite part of Michael John Carley's book *Asperger's from the Inside Out* (2008) is the dedication to his wife. It reads "for Kathryn, who rebuilt the world." I was very lonely at the time I read it and it gave me hope that someone with Asperger's could find true love. This is why I dedicated this book to my current partner. I was going to dedicate it to the many AS women in the trenches whom I admire, but the person who literally turned the lights on in my heart and my world is my partner Mike.

To find him, I stopped wishing for someone I used to have, and I stopped thinking about what I didn't want. Instead I used a simple but powerful visualization technique. I wrote a list of traits of the man I wanted as if I already had him. I started the list with "I have the perfect partner" and then went on to list his characteristics, *always speaking in the present tense.* I didn't include anything negative, as in things I didn't want, only positive things I did want. Two weeks later, he found me. Whether or not you believe in the magic of visualization, writing this list crystallizes and clarifies what traits are really going to make us happy, as opposed to what traits we think we should want in a man.

I cannot tell you how to have a good marriage but I can tell you this—don't say "yes" to the first man who asks you. I am not the only Aspergirl who got married because I had a decent boyfriend and I was of a certain age. Don't assume that you will never fall in love because you haven't yet. When it hits, you don't see it coming, and if you're already married, you'll regret it. Being in love is definitely one of the crucial components of a satisfying marriage.

Equally crucial is having a partner who *gets* AS and who doesn't want to change you, but instead wants to make things easier and more comfortable for you.

ADVICE TO PARENTS

There isn't too much you can do in this department—she will marry who she wants. Hopefully she will find someone who assuages her anxiety, not increases it. The best thing you can do is to interview the guy and see if he really understands her limitations as well as her potential. Impress upon him that there are special needs that cannot be ignored just because she's intelligent and independent. The self-esteem you've raised her to have will help her to make the right choice.

CHAPTER *13*

HAVING CHILDREN

Some of us want the companionship and love of a family while others live in fear of it; if we can barely take care of ourselves how shall we support another human being? Having children should never be entered into lightly whether or not one has Asperger's. But when one does, all the inherent issues are compounded. Having kids means saying goodbye to peace, quiet and solitude, our favorite things. There are social functions we'll have to attend, from school plays to play dates to parent–teacher meetings. We'll be expected to be caretakers; to be mature adults who make mature decisions, to be selfless; all things we might struggle with. We won't look like most other mothers, act like other mothers or feel particularly motherly. The very name "Mom" is something we may balk against, for it denotes a one-size-fits-all picture of womanhood that doesn't fit us.

> I am avoidant of marriage and having children. I don't want to be out of control of my own body. I don't want to have to be "switched on" at all times as a mother. (Kes)

> I do not have children, and I do not intend to. I wouldn't want to be responsible for raising a child. I have a hard time keeping track of myself as it is. (Shannon)

I loved being pregnant; I felt so beautiful. I loved nursing my babies. I enjoyed enriching their language and world-view. I had three children. Other parents often asked me to watch their children, too. (Widders)

I've often said that the whole teddy bear and balloon image of infancy that we find on everything from wallpapers to announcement cards should be replaced with urine, excrement, vomit, and blood, for that is what giving birth to another human being was about. It wasn't pretty, it wasn't fun, and having a baby messed with every sensory, social, and control issue I ever had. In addition, I was a pretty self-absorbed person, and having to subjugate my own needs to address another's first, was something I did not like. On one occasion my daughter and I were on a train from California to New York, when she was just two years old. She was playing with a boy and the boy's grandmother looked at our two cherubs and asked rhetorically, "Don't you just love being a mother?" I honestly and bluntly replied, "No, I don't." For a moment the woman got a look of sheer horror on her face, as she slid her bottom further from me, and over to the seat by the window, where she craned her gaze as far away from me as possible. Clearly she had just put me in the category of serial killer. I laughed to myself, and wondered at the ability of some people to lie to themselves.

She didn't ask me if I loved my daughter. If she had, I'd have said yes. It was being a mother I disliked, for I found it ridiculously demanding. From the moment she came out, screaming, tugging at my flesh, breaking the stillness of my small San Francisco apartment, filling it with horrible smells, my baby was an Aspergirl's worst nightmare. I laugh as I write this because she knows how much I love her, and knowing my sensory issues, she is now quick to turn off the music before speaking or to shush the dogs when I'm writing. But when she was a baby, I couldn't even watch a film without her crying or screaming, which violates rule 14 of the Aspie code of ethics: *thou shalt not interrupt my movie!*

In a strange twist of irony, my daughter is not autistic, but she was very un-cuddly as an infant and toddler. She was the one person I wanted to hug but she pushed me away, and when she did so, my attachment to her decreased. I became very Spock-like in my attitude to child-raising, and I don't mean Dr. Spock. I erroneously assumed that she did not need or even love me. I thought her father, who by this time had left me, might be more to her liking. For a time I left her in his care, until my strong feelings of connectedness to her returned. When they did, it was very powerful and sudden. My daughter says that she experienced a similar detachment and revival of feelings towards me at virtually the same time. I had moved overseas and she was sent to live with me.

> I have a son, age ten. He lives with his father in a town far away. He visits me 5–6 times a year. I think that is for the best. I love him, he is the joy and meaning of my life. (Siv)

When my daughter returned to my care I was, once again, a very devoted mother and a good caregiver. Despite eccentricities, my need for ritual and routine meant that things were fairly conservative, safe and predictable in our house. When we got into a schedule and a flow, it lasted for a long time and my daughter was able to settle in. I enjoyed being a single mom more than a married one, because I didn't have to share control with anybody.

> I'm happy, single, have a two-year-old son; a fantastic relationship with him. Wouldn't want to be with anyone. Motherhood is the best thing in the world. (Kylli)

Our need for control, sensory issues, and our love for learning usually means that our children read or get read to a lot, and a limited amount of television. Our sensitivity to foods and additives means that they eat nutritiously, with little junk. They get exercise and fresh air. From what I've learned from other

Aspergirls is that we make unconventional yet conservative moms; strict, safe, logical, protective, and intellectually stimulating.

As a result of control issues and distrust of school systems, we may want to home-school our children. Later in my daughter's life, when she was age seven, I home-schooled her for six months because she was not intellectually challenged at our local village school in North Wales. We started every day with *Bewitched*, followed by singing lessons and art. But we also covered all necessary subjects including math, reading, writing, geography, social studies, and science. My daughter was a straight A student once back in school. Of course, it had to be the best school, with the friendliest, most creative atmosphere I could find, not just what was convenient. At one point I took four buses a day across town to get her there and back while I was juggling university and part-time work. Other Aspergirls I talked to home-schooled their kids as well or were active in their education.

> I was smart enough but never got the help that I needed.
> I am now home-schooling my three AS boys. (Naga Empress)

Despite trying very hard, I always had the sense that what I was doing was never enough. Pre-AS awareness, my daughter had to witness my many transformations. As I was trying to figure myself out, she had to go on that journey with me, since my spiritual journey often took physical form. She had visited or lived in 14 countries by the time she was 14 years old. Other mothers had more money, more patience, more stability, and never seemed as stressed as me. They talked to each other in playgrounds, they met each other for coffee. I was never invited.

Once my daughter cried "Why can't you be normal like other moms?" That hurt. I'd been singing opera very loudly in the car. Apparently other moms didn't do that.

On the positive side, having an emotionally immature but smart mom meant that my daughter had someone to play with; someone to not only watch *Chitty Chitty Bang Bang* with, but to sing all the songs as well. It meant we moved to New Zealand because we loved the scenery in Lord of the Rings. When she was a teenager, we shared clothes. We listened to much of the same alternative music. But then she grew up and I didn't. I still watch kid's movies and sing the songs, but I do it by myself now.

She is now at college and far away, completely on her own. There is a part of me that knows she benefited from having an Aspie mom. There's another part that wishes I'd had a diagnosis and some support so that she might have had more geographic and financial stability. But I think I did a good job. She is compassionate, would never bully, has a wonderful open-minded outlook on life, is pretty nonjudgmental and is very good at social skills. That she definitely did not get from me. I am living for myself again and I have to say I like it!

While most Aspergirls I spoke with also don't have a particular affection for babies, the ones that did have children loved them very much and many found great joy, friendship, and camaraderie in their kids.

> I have no feelings of motherhood but I love my two children. (Sam)

Their house is a muse-um, when people come to see-'em, they really are a scre-am, the Aspie Family. I've never been in the household of an entirely spectrum family but I should imagine it would be a great place, filled with evidence of esoteric interests, models of our galaxy, books stacked to the ceiling, and animals running rampant.

> At the beach or park, we dig in the sand (or dirt), explore around and just do whatever makes us feel calm and happy. At Nana's, we play games with the numerous cousins, sing and dance. (Dame Kev)

> We explored the woods, dissected electronics we dragged home from the dump, and examined road kill. We went to

museums, made costumes, and started a 4-H club for dog training. We read each other to sleep every night. I was a stay at home mom for 12 years and I loved every minute of it. I am responsible, but very immature and hanging out with kids is a great way to pass time. (Widders)

Having more than one Aspergian in the house compounds some of the issues.

I thought my son was going to give me a kiss on the cheek and instead he pulled my face to his and bit me on the top lip. (He's seen me my husband kissing me and I think he misunderstood.) In a way, there was a double meltdown. He had a meltdown because I screamed at the top of my lungs and flailed around. He ran into his room and raged among his toys. I cried, went into the kitchen and tossed a bunch of leftovers from the fridge onto the floor. I went into a corner of the kitchen and rocked for a minute when I realized what I'd done. After a few minutes, he brought in one of the toys that calms both of us down and we played together for a little bit before I cleaned stuff up and got him ready for bed. (Dame Kev)

Some of us thrive in our families, and in our protective environment…and as stated can have surprisingly conservative and traditional outlooks on family. So what happens if the marriage ends? Losing the support of our partner is a shock to any mother, but in our case, we may lose the family's sole breadwinner, our all-important social and environmental buffer, and the one who took care of all the things we could not. We now have to be both mommy and daddy, with all that encompasses.

My husband was a lawyer. He left me with the kids and little money (later he took them from me). Meanwhile another man "fell in love" with me. Months later, I had twins, a boy and a girl, but he left too. I was now a single mother of five, with no job experience who now had to work for a living. By the time I got home from work, I was not up to the challenge of motherhood. I have spent the last 16 years trying to pull my life back together. I think one can say that I am a fabulous mother in a vacuum, but I really suck in real life. (Widders)

Our struggles with our children do not end when they reach adulthood. They can still push our autistic buttons and be some of the most demanding people in our lives. Even though they know we're autistic, they still want us to be parents and to meet their needs.

Generally one of my children (ages 29, 27, 21, two 16s), will start demanding something from me that I can't give them and they won't let up. I ask for privacy but they follow me through the house into my bedroom. They won't leave me alone and I get so wound up until I finally totally flip out. Anybody else, I can generally escape from. Don't think badly of my children. They are capable and bright, but they all have such strong personalities. They blame me for everything that went wrong in my marriage with their father. Because I lost so much in the fight, they think I am incompetent; because I ended up so poor, they think I am low class. He took them from me and wouldn't even let me have supervised visitation for years. It was terrible and my children have a lot to work through. They thought I was bad, but they are learning more about me now. (Widders)

The dichotomy of being emotionally immature yet intellectually sound; of being logical and regimented yet having executive dysfunction, is something that is difficult for others (social workers and Family Court judges for example) to get their heads around. We are at times suspected of being bad parents. A few of the women I spoke to had been investigated by Child Protective Services. At least two had their children temporarily taken away based on suspicion of inadequate parenting only, not on any evidence. Both were exonerated of any wrong-doing.

ADVICE TO ASPERGIRLS

We are lucky to live in a world where it is no longer unusual or undesirable to be a single lady or a childless couple. Don't worry about justifying your choices to anyone—it's your life. For those of you who do want a family, a few words of caution: Remember that having a built-in universe is great for a while. But those children will grow up and they will move on, especially if they do not inherit your Asperger's. While you will probably like the idea of being able to live for yourself once again, if you have relied too heavily on them for companionship and meaning in your life, you will be left completely without a social circle. This is empty nest syndrome taken to the nth degree and can be quite devastating. All of a sudden you have no one to watch films with, or go shopping with, etc. You then realize how alone you've allowed yourself to become. Unless you are totally happy being totally alone, try to find some friends before that happens.

If you think you do want children and don't have them yet, research very carefully what that will mean financially, socially, sensorially, and emotionally.

If you do have children, remember that if they are nonautistic they might have expectations that you do not naturally understand or anticipate. For example, it was pointed out to me *after* the fact that I should have gone out of my way to see my daughter in her prom dress or help her move into her dorm room. Both times I assumed my presence was neither wanted nor needed. There have been a myriad of instances in our lives where I simply did not know what was expected of me. And because I do not have girlfriends and am not close with my sisters or mother, I have had no one to tell me what I "should" do on such occasions. Seek help and advice from nonautistic women if you have nonautistic children. They may give you more insight into some of the milestones and events that your child might want you to acknowledge and commemorate.

Also, don't forget the hugs. Even if you don't like to hug, find a way that works for you. It is so important.

ADVICE TO PARENTS

For those of you who are worried about grandchildren, don't. We Aspergirls can make great, if somewhat unorthodox mothers. However, if you see there are "gaps" in the parenting services we provide, for example if we don't see the necessity of spending $100 every two months on hair appointments and manicures, or trick bikes and hockey gear, maybe you can step in and, without guilt-tripping us, provide some of the information and encouragement we might need in order not to miss out on anything important.

Do not pressure your Aspergirl into getting married or having children if she doesn't want them. We may never have nurtured ourselves properly and may have to do quite a bit of that before we can devote ourselves to nurturing another. We might just not want those things, full stop. And there's too much at stake to go into motherhood or marriage half-heartedly.

14

RITUAL AND ROUTINE, LOGICAL AND LITERAL THINKING, BLUNTNESS, EMPATHY, AND BEING MISUNDERSTOOD

The DSM-IV (Diagnostic and Statistical Manual of Mental Disorders, 4th edn.) says that we have a rigid adherence to nonfunctional *rituals and routines*. I guess that depends on your idea of function. The Aspergian need for R&R—ritual and routine—is a way of controlling our world. It is our security blanket; knowing what to expect, where to expect it, and who to expect it from. Whether by eating the same foods each day, taking the same route to work, lining underwear up by color in a drawer: these things make us feel safe on an otherwise precarious planet.

This need for ritual and routine is simplistically labeled as having "control issues" when an observer doesn't know a person is autistic. Saying someone has control issues sounds like an accusation—it connotes a psychological neurosis that has an incident or incidents at its base and is within our control to change or get rid of. This implies that if we just do the work we can eliminate the need for control. We *can* lessen our need for rituals and routines, with mindfulness, therapy, and effort but it will never be gone completely. We need others to understand and tolerate this.

Because Aspergirls are smart, creative, even at times outgoing, it is sometimes easy to forget that they have Asperger's. It is also easy to forget that Asperger's is mild autism. Sometimes we crave people, human contact, and even spontaneity. But, most of the time, we want to organize, straighten, engage in our rituals. Most of us spent far more time as children organizing our toys than actually playing with them. Like autistic Joan Crawfords running around yelling "No wire hangers, ever!" we need to control our world and everything in it. Hence the necessity of routine, without which there is chaos and the unexpected. We might not have a script or a backup plan for a surprise ordeal.

> As a child I needed everything to be straight and ordered or it felt unsafe. Surprises terrified me. (Pokégran)

Our reaction to being sidetracked from our rituals and routines can run the gamut from annoyance to panic to full-blown meltdown. Our lack of spontaneity can affect our relationships negatively—we can be proverbial sticks in the mud. Adherence to ritual can keep us from taking jobs, going on trips, attending functions, and having relationships. On a positive note, needing to have routine is one of the things that make us reliable—and can pay dividends at work, school, and at home, where we need to help provide stability to our family or social group.

> My job can be very repetitive; that has never bothered me. It bothers me more when my routine at work gets changed. (Elfinia)

> The need for a routine was a good thing that kept me focused on getting through college and off to work on time, so it helped my professional life. (Ann Marie)

Many nonautistics will have the same need, and as usual we are talking about a matter of degrees—frequency, necessity, and intensity. Most nonautistics would not wake up in the night hyperventilating because their flip-flops are missing, but we will. It is not the cost, it's just that they are not where they belong. Practical routines such as always putting your keys in the same place help minimize confusion. That way, we don't have to quickly look for something when we need it which can make someone with visual issues dizzy. Other rituals are more obtrusive, seem nonsensical, and fall into the realm of obsessive compulsive disorder (OCD). I had a friend with AS who had to keep his hair wet at all times—even when we went out to dinner, which meant getting up and going to the loo frequently and returning with dripping water raining down from his head onto horrified diners. None of the females I interviewed had these sorts of compulsions; ours were more innocuous. This is another way females are less conspicuous—our routines, like our obsessions, tend to be pragmatic.

We have some ability to reason with ourselves, to make compromises. Those of us who have children, for example, learn that our pristine apartments will be in disarray for much of the time and although we may not love it, we love our children, so we make that trade-off. Aspergirls may sacrifice some of that much needed alone time to have love, sex, and companionship. How much we can trade may have to do with how far along on the spectrum we are, and also a myriad of other factors, like personality traits and past experiences.

Many of my meltdowns are caused from a change in routine. I cannot handle change. (Brandi)

I drive my son to school and then I have six hours to paint on my own. I eat the same foods each day and everything has Asian chili sauce on it. I email people and pursue my special interests. I may ring my mother. Every day is the same. (Camilla)

Our rigidity extends to our thinking and indeed *literal thinking* is another hallmark of our syndrome. We have to train the people we interact with about our need for exactitude. If someone tells us they are going to call at 6pm and they don't call until 6:30 this could be very upsetting. We might spend the entire half hour wondering if they got killed or abducted, for why would someone not keep their word? We may call them in lieu of waiting. This can lead others to think that we are controlling and insecure.

Literal thinking means that sometimes I am really dense. I once had a recipe for some vegetarian dish that called for a garnish of 12 kalamata olives. I went to the deli counter at my supermarket and ordered 12 olives. The man put a scoopful into a little plastic container and asked, "That look right?" And I said, "I don't know, how many are in there?" He looked at me angrily and then counted them. *18.* "Take six out please, I only need 12." It didn't occur to me that I could just eat the other six. He sighed heavily as he removed the six extra olives. I was embarrassed and uncomfortable, but I didn't know why. I was only doing what the recipe told me to do.

> The taxi driver pulled into my street and asked "Where are you?" I answered from the back seat "I'm right here."
> (Hope)

People either think we're messing with them because we seem intelligent, or else they think we're not so smart after all. Humor in particular can be lost on us. Why can we understand everything from Shakespeare to South Park, yet not realize that when a person says their underwear is brown they're only joking? We're either overanalyzing, so have missed the joke or point by misdirection, or else we sometimes assume people wouldn't bother to joke about such things. This often appears as no sense of humor, but while some Aspergirls have told me jokes are wasted on them I do not think this is the majority. The brain is a flexible organ and our sense of humor, like every other skill, can be cultivated and refined.

Blunt, honest speech is another thing that can get us into trouble. We try to explain ourselves clearly but it seems to backfire. Aspergirls don't understand that the world wants their honesty wrapped in tact. Our tact skills tend to be at chop*sticks* level, not Chop*in*.

> I have made enemies because I say what I mean and don't dress it up in the acceptable flowery or bureaucratic jargon. But being a journo basically gives me social permission to be blunt, direct, and ask odd questions. (Polly)

> Many, many, many times I have been very misunderstood because of my frankness and my honesty. I have learned to withhold my opinion a bit in the last few years. Being misunderstood causes me great pain. (Camilla)

All but one of the Aspergirls interviewed said they are frequently *misunderstood*. This takes the form of having our words and/or intentions misread, and having autistic behaviors misinterpreted, causing unintended offense. We may be accused of something we haven't done, at least not intentionally, and are probably not even capable of. To give an example, our social avoidance and withdrawal can lead others to believe that we have something to hide. A few years ago, I was evicted from a house I was renting because the landlady, who lived next door, misinterpreted my spacey behavior as a drug problem, which could not have been further from the truth as I don't take anything harder than ibuprofen. Mild autism is almost always misunderstood, and the resultant "filling in the blanks" can seriously hurt our reputations, cause us to lose jobs, friends, homes, and more.

> I nearly failed my nursing placement as people thought I was arrogant, argumentative and egotistical. I was devastated to find I had offended them. (Kylli)

Because we have a childish innocence but a woman's body, when we are open and friendly, we are often accused of flirting. Lack of eye contact means we must be lying. Because we're always trying to figure out the game, and set things up in advance, we may seem manipulative. Our high levels of anxiety equals neurotic and controlling...*bitchy*.

> Often I will find out much later that something I said was taken the wrong way. I was also accused of lying throughout my childhood, though I was more truthful than either of my siblings. I have been accused of manipulation where it was not intended, too. (Shannon)

Small children, whether autistic or not, feel misunderstood and this is very upsetting to them. While nonautistic kids grow out of it, because we don't emotionally mature, we don't. The feeling continues and eventually, over a lifetime, can cause us to retreat from the world, giving up on trying to have friends or jobs. Why should we try, when we know we're just going to be misunderstood? Unchecked, this can lead to bitterness, which I find tragic in so gifted and innately idealistic a population.

> I try to explain myself very clearly, but I seem to experience things in a completely different way from most people. (Heather)

Empathy is another area where we are misread. It is thought that people with Asperger's lack empathy. When our empathy is functional, which can be much of the time, it is so strong that it can be overwhelming. Perhaps that is why we may almost prefer the alternative.

> At times I have empathy...and I also have a sense of feeling *too* much. Yet, I have frequently been accused of being insensitive. I always feel inside as if I care deeply about others, but this is not always perceived or understood. (Camilla)

Empathy is similar to compassion or sympathy depending on what dictionary you go to. It may be hard to define but we know when it is lacking. In our case, it will be absent for one of a couple of reasons—either 1) *because we feel it but don't know how to express it*; 2) *because we can't relate to a situation*—i.e. it's something we've never experienced before so we don't know how it feels, or 3) *because we feel attacked so we shut down to self-protect.*

> I sometimes feel bad for people in bad situations but unless it is something that has happened to me or that I can directly relate to I have trouble relating and feeling as bad as I maybe should for them. (Nikki)

We are logical beings who try to be genuine. We are blunt. The result is we won't often say what others want and expect to hear. We process things differently and in our own time.

> I had an uncle who killed himself and I never cried for his loss, not once. He was miserable in his life and he was always talking about leaving this planet. So, I've never been sure if feeling nothing was so wrong. Maybe I had said goodbye so many times already, that I didn't need to in real life? I remember after he died my mom just started screaming at me that "I was so cold" and "dead inside" because I hadn't mourned…those words still haunt me. I often wonder if she was right. I sometimes worry I'm a sociopath. I don't seem to feel what others do. I lie and say I do, when I just feel numb. (Elfinia)

I believe that most people with Asperger's start out life very sensitive. As we get hurt and misread by others, time and again, we get better and better at shutting empathy off, which we'll talk about more in Chapter 18.

> There is a person at my work, who I have strong antipathy for. Recently it was known that she has a lethal condition, and will die soon. Others take that in perspective, but I

can't feel anything else for her than before. She is just as hard to stand as ever. (Siv)

I usually make the first move as far as feeling a little empathy. If the person is unwilling to show it to me back, depending on the situation, I will get angry. I tend to forgive, but if the lack of caring on their part continues, any feeling of empathy towards that person completely disappears. It may seem extreme, but if I saw them about to get run over by a truck, I would do nothing. It's not a sense of revenge, it's a blankness. I don't know how else to explain it, but the feeling is like that person is sort of non-existent, like a shadow. A walking, talking shadow. On the flipside, if a person makes a positive effort to show me a little compassion, I tend to defend that person no matter what. (Dame Kev)

ADVICE TO ASPERGIRLS

Regarding rituals and routines—shake it up. Try new foods, new clothes, new restaurants, new routes, new TV shows. Try a new approach to making friends, new topics of conversation, new classes or areas of study. Try it, you might (gasp!) like it. Of course we revert to our root passions, interests and routines, but we do pick up new ones along the way. If you cannot do it on your own, behavioral therapy can help you break routines a little at a time. If your rituals are more obtrusive, if they are more like perseveration, then you need to first try exercise, and something like yoga to calm your mind and release the energy you are feeling throughout your body. I've used reiki and reflexology on people with Asperger's and they tell me it has relaxed them for a period of time afterward. Reiki is beginning to be studied in controlled academic environments and early results are positive.

If your need for ritual and routine is a way to make you feel safe, you might want to journal your fears, talk about them with a counselor or someone you trust, and even give your spirituality some thought. In a world which is hard to navigate because of sensory processing disorders, spatial issues, coordination, and anxiety, we have to learn to rely on our higher sense and trust— both in our own abilities and in the ability of the universe to provide for us what we need.

Admitting you have little tact is actually quite liberating. Give yourself scope to screw up and you won't get so devastated when you do. I am still often misunderstood, but of course being "out" I use disclosure and education to inform people of what my intentions and actions are really all about. I now go out into the world knowing full well I will probably be misread, but at least I don't get angry at people anymore because of it. Tact is a fine art. Approach it the same way you would approach learning a new dance. Pay attention to your steps and practice not stepping on any toes.

There is a visual metaphor I use in my lectures which I have contrived to help me be less direct and to make my words more acceptable to others. We tend to be archers when it comes to verbal communication—direct and to the point. If you picture your words as an arrow, then you can also picture how the receiver might flinch or recoil when those words hit them. Instead, gift wrap your words in pretty paper (tact) and hand them to your recipient. They will receive it with an open attitude (take your words on board).

One thing that nobody likes is a know-it-all. There is a difference between being smart and being a smart-ass. Having faith in your intelligence is not the same as flaunting it—*I* know you don't, but others may think you do. If you combine intelligence with tact, you are more likely to get what you want out of a situation. Intelligence *minus* tact usually results in not getting what you want; or getting it but losing something in the process, such as a potential friend.

Being misunderstood seems to be at the root of most of our challenges. Apart from disclosure, letting others in involves striking a balance: you have to care enough to try and interact, and give yourself *and others* room to make mistakes, so that if and when you are misunderstood you're neither surprised nor devastated. Find a good friend, even if it is just one, who really and truly gets you.

Empathy skills too can be learned. While many of us love to watch films and get very caught up in the lives and dramas of the various characters, most of us have a difficult time relating at length to people talking about their trials and tribulations. A trick I have is to use my love of films to learn how to empathize with others. As someone is talking to me about their situation I make a "mini-movie'—I picture the characters and action in my head. I'll give an example. My mother has been telling me about a woman she works with who loves her dog so much she brings it to work in a baby stroller, for it is old and sickly. The dog has just died. I feel nothing for the woman at first, because I have never seen her or her dog. I make a mini-movie in my head, put myself and my dog in the starring roles and then I can understand how she must feel. My mind becomes engaged and my heart opens up. If I didn't make a conscious effort to do that, if her words just stayed in my head, they would make me uncomfortable, triggering a nervous, "I need to stim" feeling. If I let it down to my heart through those methods, I feel some sympathy and feel better about myself. I think this is what my Aspergirls have been saying about having better sympathy than empathy…personally I find the distinction vague—the important thing is to learn to *care*.

Learn the fine art of listening. You often don't have to *do* anything, it is the mere act of listening that people need and want from another human being. That is something that I think most of us with AS have a hard time with—not being able to do anything about what we hear, so therefore we don't want to hear because it seems to be a waste of everyone's time.

ADVICE TO PARENTS

Respect the rituals, but make an agreement with your child to try one new food/book/activity, etc. once a week or so. Even your grownup daughter needs to be both challenged and respected in this regard. Do understand that if she really doesn't like something, it is not a good idea to criticize or cajole her—don't tell her to "lighten up"; it'll only make her blood boil! She needs her R&R to feel safe and secure. If rituals are truly nonsensical and repetitive there are therapies, exercise, and of course, there is medication. But first try finding an outlet for that anxiety, something she will enjoy, an alternative to a repetitive activity that might be more constructive. It could be music, science, art, hiking, you may have to try several things before you find the right one.

If your girl seems unsympathetic or unfeeling at times, the best thing to do is not to tell her how she *should* feel, but give her a similar example or incident from her own life that she can relate to. You will see the lights go on.

A positive hand will help your Aspergirl learn tact a lot quicker than being admonished. Her tactlessness is unintentional 99 percent of the time. If you have AS yourself, you'll know how it all works, but if you don't, it's so hard to understand how such an intelligent person can be unaware of some of the implications of things she says. Use my visual metaphor or find one of your own, to help with her "delivery" and don't use criticism or embarrass her—she will be upset if she feels she has upset someone else. Learn to value her directness and her honesty.

CHAPTER 15

DIAGNOSIS, MISDIAGNOSIS AND MEDICATION

The problems with diagnosis of Asperger syndrome are the high cost, the lack of insurance here in America, how it is often not covered by insurance anyway, as well as its subjective nature—there is no blood test to confirm autism or Asperger's. Word is, the DSM-V (Diagnostic and Statistical Manual of Mental Disorders, 5th Edn., due out in 2013) is going to eliminate AS as a separate diagnosis and include it under the autism umbrella. The water is muddy and shall remain so. Three different doctors may decide what you have based on their experience and knowledge—and knowledge of female AS is limited. Hans Asperger described the symptoms in boys, so doctors don't know what to look for. Fortunately that is beginning to change, but slowly.

> I think females are *very* different from the males and it is the males that all the literature is based on. It leads to misdiagnosis of the women and of course, they then don't receive the right services. (Dr. Barbara Nichols, Adult Asperger's Association, Tucson, AZ)

Receiving a diagnosis of Asperger's always "feels right" to the recipient. I've never interviewed a person diagnosed with AS who said it didn't seem to fit. I have, however, encountered many people who received several *other* diagnoses throughout their lives, and each time, they felt it only covered part of the picture, either because it was focusing on one aspect of Asperger's (e.g. physical tics) or because the doctor was noticing the comorbid condition (e.g. bipolar depression). The unfortunate result of this is that the Aspergirl is often given medication, either for a condition she doesn't have, or for a comorbid symptom, while not getting the support she needs for Asperger's. This is to the detriment of her health, happiness and even her financial stability.

> I've been misdiagnosed with everything from schizophrenia to multiple personalities via bipolar. I've been on every antidepressant you've ever heard of. I was diagnosed AS at 25, after a shrink ran every test in the world to try to prove I *didn't* have it. It was such a relief. (Polly)

Misdiagnosis means that we're not receiving the right advice for coping with work, college, life, relationships, and everything else. In some cases it threatens our sanity and our lives.

> I was at university at the time, and having a real struggle. I was trying so hard to be normal; to be social, to have friends and study groups, go to activities, stay near the top of my class. I exhausted my body and mind to the point that they crashed. I consulted a doctor at the university health center. The doctor talked to me for 15 minutes and handed me a bagful of Paxil samples. Four days after, I had the uncontrollable urge to take a knife and cut myself with it. I was then put on anti-psychotics, SSRIs (selective serotonin reuptake inhibitors), anti-convulsants, and mood stabilizers. It was an absolute nightmare. When they started me on anti-psychotics I began hallucinating; I heard voices *commanding* me to cut myself. It was really frightening. It never occurred to me

that the voices were being caused by the medication; I thought I had gone crazy. I landed in the hospital after a suicide attempt with a diagnosis of schizo-affective disorder.

After getting off *all* the meds two years later, the need to cut disappeared. The voices went away too, and have never come back. Getting off medication solved a whole fistful of problems then and there. Eventually, a couple of observant therapists in the anxiety group I was attending finally put the pieces together and arrived at Asperger's. Now I take a carefully balanced cocktail of vitamins and minerals to help my body and mind be as stable as possible. (Heather)

Many women do not find out that they have Asperger's and have never even heard of it, until their children (usually sons) are diagnosed and the doctor looks to the parents to find the source.

I was misdiagnosed several times: mentally challenged, ADHD, manic depressive (based on my meltdowns and zone outs). Next it was Tourette's (at age 13), based on hand flapping, double speaking words under my breath, the inability to keep focused on a person's face and the occasional sound outburst. The AS diagnosis for me didn't come until after both of my sons were diagnosed with autism. (Dame Kev)

It wasn't until our third child was evaluated; my husband and I started to see similarities with our kids and ourselves. I knew that I was always different and I felt a relief to have a diagnosis. (Jen)

More misdiagnoses than I can list…They tried various mind meds but I react badly to all. When a teacher thought my youngest two were autistic, I thought "Nonsense, they are just like me" and so I read all about it to prove the teacher wrong. Instead I realized that most of my family are on the spectrum. Diagnosis proved it. (Pokégran)

Others, including myself, were trying to figure out the underlying cause of our partner's strange habits when we stumbled upon the A-word for the first time. Then we realized that we had some similar attributes. It was through a small piece about females in a book primarily about males that I first found evidence that I might be on the spectrum. The portrayal of Isabelle (the fictionalized version of Mary Newport) in the 2005 film *Mozart and the Whale* clinched it. It was only after I'd watched the film several times that I realized—*she is so much like me*. From there, I delved into *everything* I could find.

Those of us who don't have Asperkids really have to go through a process of elimination with our doctors. Who can afford *that* without free healthcare or really good insurance? Self-diagnosis is sometimes the only affordable, practical alternative—and it is usually accurate. Several of the women self-diagnosed first, and then received an official verdict later, after searching, saving, and battling their insurance provider.

I am undiagnosed, as I have no health insurance (surprise!), but when I was younger I was diagnosed with social anxiety disorder, generalized anxiety disorder, OCD, and depression. Those all fit my struggles but I feel they do not cover everything. Asperger syndrome feels like the complete diagnosis. (Elle)

I self-diagnosed in 2008, officially diagnosed with AS in February 2009. (Rachel)

When I called a local neuropsychologist to discuss with her the possibility of getting an adult diagnosis, she said she'd only diagnosed children and she seemed to have a very limited, vague awareness of AS, much less adult female AS. She told me that she'd interview family as part of the process. I called a few more. Most said they'd only diagnose children, while those that did adults would also insist on the family interview. While some Aspergirls are lucky enough to have supportive, *observant* mothers, others were physically, emotionally, or even sexually abused by family members. To include them in our process is not something we want to put ourselves through. The same ability to deceive oneself enough to beat or abuse a child—or turn a blind eye—is going to be the same *in*ability to recall details correctly.

> I was not diagnosed until I was almost 21, so it was not known that I had any form of autism until that time. Looking back, I was certainly different. I threw a lot of fits, got in a lot of fights; I was sexually abused by my older brother. My parents would not acknowledge my diagnosis until recently. (Shannon)

> I was being sexually abused by my father but was always told I was lying. Family always told me to "be normal." Only recently diagnosed. (Bramble)

Older Aspergirls' parents are now in their seventies or eighties (if they're still alive), and even if they were good parents, they may not have the power of recall. Back in our younger days, parents tended to put their children out of doors from dawn till dusk, and barely knew where they were half the time. People just didn't concern themselves with their children's inner processes unless external signs were obvious. As long as there were no broken bones, and supper was on the table, everything was fine.

Sometimes even after correct diagnosis, other practitioners will dispute its legitimacy or its scope.

> Most of the practitioners I have spoken to about the Asperger's diagnosis just don't believe it, as they see me as a functioning adult who is capable of carrying out activities of daily living. (Brandi)

Many doctors and health professionals have a negative perception of Asperger's and dole our the verdict as if it is a death sentence.

> She stated that no medication will help me unless I take large amounts and many of them and have the doctors put me in a "coma." She also said that based on my previous history of employment I would probably "end up slicing my wrists" depending on the job I pick. My impression from her response is that I would be better off locked in a closet for the rest of my life. (Brandi)

Fortunately for all, this attitude and lack of knowledge about AS is changing, and many professionals are working very hard to try and understand the signs, symptoms, positives, and complexities of our syndrome.

ADVICE TO ASPERGIRLS

I said this in *22 Things* (Simone 2009)—in addition to the burden of having Asperger's, you also have the burdens of: getting a diagnosis; getting follow-up advice and support; and you may always have to try and convince people and practitioners to believe you and the diagnosing physician.

If the diagnosis didn't fit, then you could cast it aside (apart from the fact it will be on your medical records, and god knows what American insurance companies and some employers will think of it). But I have never met an Aspie or Aspergirl who said it didn't. If it does fit, then use the information you find in books, on the internet, and from therapists and support groups to help yourself. If you're not diagnosed, at least you won't be turned down by an American insurance company for having a pre-existing condition.

Beware of doctors who are quick to throw multiple meds at you. If these cautionary tales haven't convinced you, there are more in the next chapter. Meds should be prescribed and taken responsibly, one at a time, and discontinued immediately if their side effects are bad. Read Temple Grandin's *Thinking in Pictures* (2006) for her scientific and sensible approach to administering medication.

ADVICE TO PARENTS

There are good doctors and bad doctors. Doctors knowledgeable about AS and those who are not. There are physicians who are open-minded and those who have tunnel-vision. They are just people, not gods. They are also as numerous as dandelions in the field. Find one you like, trust, and respect. They should be willing to take your concerns and theories on board. They should not be dismissive of your thoughts or your daughter's self-diagnosis, for no one knows her life experience better than she, and following that, probably yourself, *if* you're an observant, hands-on parent. Once the diagnosis is procured, make AS your passionate study. Don't just stop there, or life will be difficult for her. Very difficult. You must become active in learning and participating in her development. Be part of the solution or you will be part of the problem.

CHAPTER *16*

DEPRESSION MELTDOWNS, PTSD, AND MORE ABOUT MEDS

According to the psychiatrist Thomas Szasz, *there are no psychological disorders, only "problems in living"* (2008). Aspergirls have had more than their fair share of life problems. While having AS often results in depression, PTSD, and other symptoms, these are not an inevitability. True understanding—and acceptance—of our differences by friends, family, teachers, and peers will diminish those problems dramatically.

Depression is triggered by feeling powerless—powerless to bring love, money, friends, health, understanding, or other things into your life. With the exception of some of life's more extreme occurrences—death of a loved one, for example, most of those things can be returned into one's control, by finding new solutions to old problems.

The term "chemical imbalance" has been bandied about for the last few decades, to try and sell us the antidepressant du jour. We are more susceptible to depression when there is an imbalance in the body; but what that imbalance is in each individual would take analyzing by specialists through a variety of tests. Imbalances would more likely be corrected through a regimen of vitamins and supplements, tailored to the individual's needs, than through a one-size-fits-all psychotropic pill.

Antidepressants and other psychoactive drugs are not solutions. They treat *symptoms*, not the source. Yet doctors have been quick to prescribe them for us.

> I was once diagnosed with "double depression" where a normally depressed person becomes even more depressed; janitor must have been sitting in for the doc that day. I was briefly on Adderall; it made me go nuts. (Olive)

> When I was *eight years old*, I was tested and my mom was told that my emotions were "too strong/an overreaction"; they put me on meds that reduced anger. I think I was given too much. I couldn't feel anything. I didn't feel control over my brain. (Megan)

Some Aspergirls do find meds helpful and I don't mean to suggest you stop taking them—*if* they're working for you and *if* the benefit outweighs the risks.

> I use a lot of cognitive behavioral therapy (CBT) strategies in tandem with the Temple Grandin approach to SSRI antidepressants: ⅓ to half the normal "starter dose" as the maximum for someone with AS. It is working well, I have alleviation of comorbids and reduction in anxiety. Too high a dose, normal for others, was hideous for me. (Camilla)

There are basically two types of autistic meltdowns: *temper* meltdowns, which we'll talk about in the next chapter, and *depression* meltdowns. Temper meltdowns are usually over pretty quick and the physical fallout over in a few hours or a day. Depression meltdowns can last for days or even weeks and are incredibly crippling, intense, and debilitating. Both meltdowns can result in stomach pain, nausea, vomiting, exhaustion, dizziness, headaches, diarrhea, broken friendships or relationships, and lasting embarrassment.

If you've never had an intense depression meltdown you cannot know what it is like. I can only describe my own process from the inside out, but from what other Aspergirls tell me, we have similar experiences. A depression meltdown might start with a cloudy feeling on the edges of my brain. A tightening at the same time along the area of my forehead. I feel a little down, a little negative. I'm not breathing deep. (Sometimes however, I'm perfectly fine, happy even.) Then, there will be a trigger; some event—it might be a comment, or a change of plan. It might be after a day of social or sensory overload. It might be something more obvious like a breakup or being the object of scorn, misunderstanding, or hurtful gossip. Whatever the reason, I will feel like I've been hit with a baseball bat. I'll feel it in my belly and my head. Immediately, I'm dizzy, like the world has shifted off its axis. It's that swooning feeling right before you faint. It's the feeling you have when you receive terrible news; now freeze that and stay there for hours, days even. Once this happens, it's very hard to stop ourselves "going down the rabbit hole." We go down quickly and we go down hard. We will cry a lot, sometimes to the point of hyperventilating and choking. We will despair of anything ever being right again. We are paralyzed with grief.

> It feels like I have a black hole in my stomach that is sucking my entire body in. My insides hurt, sometimes to the extent that I make myself sick. There is nothing I can do other than curl up in a little ball and cry. This can last for hours and at times for days. It's horrible, and can be really hard to recover from. (Andi)

Depression meltdowns are like being in solitary confinement, in a dark, damp basement, full of filth and spiders. They are like death, the loneliest place on earth, the worst nightmare you've ever had come to life. They make me wonder if I'm possessed, if I am insane, if I am cursed and if I will ever be happy again. Do I need a doctor? Do I need a witch doctor to shake some sort of snake rattle over me and cast out the evil entities? Why was I chosen to feel this way? When I sleep there is no respite, for I might dream of someone murdering me with razor blades.

> I have nightmares and vivid dreams. I often dream about flying on an airplane that starts to crash, storms, someone chasing me, someone drowning, trying to call 911 but I cannot push the right numbers when dialing the phone, calling for help but I do not have a voice…I often wake up three or four times a night. (Jen)

> During the really terrible depressions, day after day I lie in bed; anguish has taken my body and my thoughts are not my own. (Brandi)

While their onset may be fairly swift, it takes ages to physically recover; in fact, the recovery process feels quite similar to that after a mutism episode. The sick, stiff, painful, frozen, numb feeling slowly dissipates and limbs, brain, and breath begin to return to normal. Every time I recover I hope to god I don't have a depression meltdown ever again, but I still do; less frequently than I used to but even once in a while is too much. It is always, at its root, something to do with losing my power; having it taken from me and feeling hopeless. Financial problems, social difficulties; these are some of the things that set us off. Also romantic issues.

While some Aspergirls are not very romantic, others are extra-so, and an unrequited love, failed hopes and expectations, a bad date, these are all things that can bring on a mega-meltdown. The kind that have us taking to our bed like a jilted Victorian bride, incapable of speech or smiling; drowning in puddles of tears, unable to think straight, or even breathe properly. We can't even read or watch a film in such a state, the usual sanctuaries for minor meltdowns or minor depressions. When such a meltdown sets in, the world is a black and evil place.

I spent the entire summer in my bed. I could hardly move. I have seen about half a dozen shrinks, and none was helpful. I recently searched for shrinks in my new area and wrote all of them to inquire if they were interested in working with Aspies. The few who responded said "no." (Widders)

How do we get help? How do we get out of it?

I get myself to a counselor or crisis center. I know if I don't sort myself out quickly, I'll get stuck in depression. I have to be able to talk to someone about my problems and have them break things down for me; I get so overwhelmed with my own emotions that I can't understand what's going on inside my own head. (Andi)

I maintain a healthy diet and I eat well and I exercise. I share on forums or at NA (Narcotics Anonymous) meetings. I see an autism specialist once a fortnight. This helps me manage the low points. I also know they will pass. (Camilla)

I firmly believe that while we are predisposed, depression is not inevitable.

I usually don't get depressed, but sometimes I get the sense that I'm standing on the edge of a cliff and I could fall into a dark place at any time. After a while, the feeling goes away. I haven't fallen off the cliff in several years. (Riley)

Even with diagnosis, it is often difficult to tell where AS ends and psychological problems begin.

I had an abusive childhood, so it is often hard for professionals to know how much of my behaviors are related to post-traumatic stress disorder (PTSD) and how much are Asperger traits. This is where my (AS) kids have helped me to learn about myself. They were not abused and demonstrate many of the same patterns and behaviors, which helps me to see where the PTSD ends and the autism begins. (Jen)

Despite rampant levels of serious depression, the majority of Aspergirls interviewed have not thought seriously of suicide. Although most of us have contemplated it, few had made any real attempts and most said it was something they could never bring themselves to do. Consideration for loved ones and fear of the unknown stopped us. Although wanting control over our selves can cause us to contemplate it, not being in control of what happens after we die is an even bigger deterrent.

It wasn't that I wanted to end it all, per se, but that I wanted to take away the "toy" they were using, which was me. (Dame Kev)

I have wished for death most every night for as long as I can remember. I slashed my arm up once trying to tell someone how depressed I was. Though it is a dark shadow that envelops my heart and keeps anything from bringing me joy, there is still the vaguest glimmer of hope that tomorrow will be better. (Bramble)

Elfinia, a devout dog lover, found one of her favorite grooming clients, a big golden retriever named Cody, dead on the floor at work after the visiting vet put him down at the owner's request. The body was then moved to a cage across from her grooming table where she had to spend her entire work day in view of his body. In tears, she put a sheet over Cody but was yelled at for doing so. The experience triggered a major depression, as it occurred on top of the stress of a new job with multiple duties.

I watched the cremation guy take Cody away. I went home numb, grabbed a kitchen knife from the drawer and filled the bath tub. My boyfriend caught me before

I got in. After that I tried therapy. I was sent from the therapist directly to the hospital, where I spent the night frightened and treated very badly by the staff. They wouldn't let me pee without someone watching. I slept on a hard plastic chair; I don't have insurance so they wouldn't give me a bed. They kept giving me Ativan (Lorazepam) for the extreme panic attacks I was having. I was interviewed by a very angry and insulting intern while being so drugged up I could hardly think. He told me I was going to be shipped off to a mental institution in another town. I was sent in a cop car to a home for the criminally insane nearly an hour away. They sent me home two hours later, after spending time in a locked room with guys sort of rubbing themselves and looking at me. All that sort of scared me straight on suicide at least, but I can't say I got any real help for it. I just don't want to go through any of that ever again. (Elfinia)

Her experience is not uncommon. To put an autistic person on the edge of a complete breakdown through something like this cannot be good medical—or human—practice.

ADVICE TO ASPERGIRLS

While approximately one-third of women and girls interviewed for this book were on antidepressants at the time and said that they were being helped, most interviewed had been on meds in the past and found them only temporarily helpful, not helpful at all, or debilitating. When you first take an antidepressant it can give a feeling of euphoria, but like the first happy buzz of a cocktail or the initial rush of infatuation, it doesn't last. Meds may be more helpful in controlling anxiety. Anxiety is part and parcel of AS but depression exists because there's a problem in your life. You can kick-start your bike with a medicine charger, but if you're still going to drive down the same old road it won't be long before you're depressed again. But, as the song says, "There's still time to change the road you're on."

Don't give your power away to anyone, even a doctor. A *good* doctor will talk to you, find out why you're depressed and what sort of support you have. If you still need/want drugs, they'll prescribe something non-addictive, with fewer side effects and risks. (*Always* investigate risks yourself.) When meds don't work properly, unwise doctors tend to just give us a different kind, and then another, sometimes rapidly changing our prescriptions which can wreak havoc with our minds. The wrong psychotropic drug can induce psychotic behavior.

Human beings need love, they need companionship (even Aspies), they need support and they need understanding. The absence of these things should indicate a need for a change in plan, a change in strategy, maybe a change in environment and who we surround ourselves with, not a need for medication. Even if we are predisposed to depression, wise choices, especially with regard to who we let into our lives, are going to prevent the circumstances which would push us over the edge.

It is easy to blame neurotypical society and discrimination for our problems and resultant depression, but I think that is only part of it. Our reactions to external triggers must be under our control. You must find a concrete, scientific solution to each and every one of your problems. Identify the source of your depression, whether it is, as Szasz says, a "problem with living," or some sort of true imbalance in your system. We must be our own body detectives *and* enlist the aid of an enlightened, cooperative professional to find strategies that work. We need to follow our bliss—for Aspergirls, that means allowing yourself to play, to work with your talents and passions. And to aggressively take steps to outsmart the zillions of sensory triggers that are all around us. It means finding those people who accept us for who we are, and actively avoiding those who don't.

Yours is a neurological, physical condition, not a spiritual one, not a psychological one, not an emotional one, although certainly problems in these areas will form if you don't get the help and support you need. Try *re-framing* each and every issue that is plaguing you. So much of life is how you look at it. Negative thinking is habit-forming and no matter how understandable it is in our case, we still want to be the ones to bring the world to a higher place, and not let it pull us down to the depths.

Holistic antidepressants

These have been known to help those with AS: 5HT-P (which sounds like a motor oil but is actually a natural supplement you can get in a vitamin shop), St. John's wort, ginkgo biloba, Valor, and more. There is no Federal Drugs Administration (FDA)-satisfying proof that these things work but you can try them yourself and see. I find a powerful antioxidant called Amrit very helpful in alleviating anxiety, leveling moods and helping me manage stress. As with any supplement or med, autistic people usually need less, so start with a ⅓ dose.

Writing

Writing is a powerful tool and has been mentioned more than once in this book. If you are not good with writing then painting, drawing, or playing an instrument are good releases as well. Don't forget to chronicle or capture your happy and positive moments, for you need to catalog the good in your life too, to remind yourself when you need it most, that you can be happy.

Video diary

This is another excellent tool. Record yourself speaking aloud your thoughts when you are in the depths and throes of depression. Let it all out. But don't put it online or publish it *anywhere* until you have viewed the recording with a clear head.

Depression is *not* who you are—it is not your whole being. It is a temporary state of mind, a temporary lens that is coloring your world and your judgment; your perception of your current reality. When you view the video(s) the day after or when you are in a better mood, you will see that some of your thoughts are not a true indication of your general or usual thinking. Others will be valid and they'll indicate real situations and frustrations. But getting depressed about those things will not solve them.

Depression does not solve money problems, romantic problems, social issues, school difficulties—depression is the *anti*-solution. When you sink into depression, you get farther and farther away from your power, and hence, from a solution. And having people feel sorry for you will not make them know how to help you. It may even make them *not* want to help you, for even those with severe depression can get blamed for it—as if they are doing it merely to get attention. No one will know the depths that you can sink to. No one will go all the way into hell with you. You have to rise up, be your own action hero, and be strong in yourself.

As soon as you feel a meltdown coming on, get proactive. Get yourself away from the situation that contains the triggers. Eat healthy food before you lose your appetite, and drink plenty of fluid. Take your regular vitamins or supplements so your body and mind aren't weakened or starving for nutrients. Get some exercise, quick! Do not take to your bed—strap on your skates or your sneakers and hit the road or the courts, whatever your exercise choice is. Sweat it off.

Comfort yourself—pet your dogs, take a hot bath, wear a soft robe. Stay far away from people who make you feel bad about yourself.

Use your visualization skills—many of you can picture things vividly and then build them. Do that with your life. Picture your life then build it. Picture your attitude then build it. Picture your happiness and strength and then build it. For those of you who have a loved one, picture yourself holding their hand (if they are not there). Hang on to that hand, pull yourself up. For those who are spiritual, picture in your mind Jesus, Buddha, or whatever your ultimate pillar of strength and safety is. Visualization is a very powerful tool but it has to be steady and consistent to be effective, so put images in your home, especially your bedroom or wherever you spend your vulnerable time; positive images that reflect who or where you want to be.

A lot of women watch sad and tearful dramas when they feel crappy—try putting on a comedy instead, as an anti-meltdown prescription.

Some of us drink to cope, but I was surprised at how many Aspergirls drink very little or not at all, nor do they do recreational drugs. This is good—these thing are depressants. They make us say things we shouldn't say, already a problem while in serious depression and meltdown.

For those of us who have someone to talk to, we must be grateful for them. For those who don't have anyone, it is very, very difficult. If you are alone, do know that it is not the end of the world and that you will find someone someday—start looking for them now. They don't have to be a lover. In many ways it is better if they are not, for that will tax your relationship. Try to find an advisor, counselor, email pal, fellow Aspie, anyone you can call or turn to when you are having a meltdown. Even someone at the end of a phone or webcam is better than no one. I know we want to be alone, but that is only self-enforcing in a way. The mirror of another soul can make us realize the depths we are sinking into before it gets too habit-forming. You don't want to get in the habit of thinking the worst and assuming you are right all the time.

Having so many challenges and hurdles to navigate can mean that your life will be fraught with some difficulty. As a result you may get used to living a life in crisis. Whether it's a social crisis, a romantic crisis, work or financial crisis, or depression crisis, be aware that living in crisis can become habitual. You may feel persecuted, unlucky, hard done by and a host of other negative emotions and mindsets. You must take back your power. Living in crisis is another way of saying that everyone and everything has power over you.

Attempting suicide gives bureaucratic institutions power over you. Don't even think about it. It means they win. As the saying goes—don't let the bastards get you down.

To young Aspergirls

I hope that you have supportive parents and family. If you don't, life can be exceptionally lonely for you. Ignorant parents are an Aspergirl's worst torture. But understand this—they don't understand how sensitive you are, and how dark that dark place is. If they knew better, they would do better. They don't realize how much they are hurting you. You will be a kind, caring person when you are older, and if you have children of your own you would never subject them to this kind of isolation. Hang on to your vision of your future. You must get as much education as you can, to get financial independence to be able to live on your own and not *need* anyone.

ADVICE TO PARENTS

Meltdowns should be replaced with healthy coping skills and depressions should be replaced with action. Too many Aspergirls are left alone in life, in their bedrooms, apartments, etc. to muddle through this thing alone. While we mature fast when we are young, we level off and it often takes longer for us to be able to leave our parents' house. If we do not get the support and understanding from you that we need, we will go into the world prematurely and will no doubt find ourselves in situations that we do not know how to handle and are not equipped to deal with.

Nothing makes a person more depressed than being blamed for it. Nothing is more annoying than hearing "get over it" or my own personal favorite, "lighten up." We need a sympathetic ear, and then some intelligent questions that will get us thinking rather than reacting. Questions like:

- What started the feeling?

- How do you feel right now?

- What do you need to begin to feel better?

- Would you like something to eat or drink?

- Would you like a hot bath, etc...?

These sorts of things show that you are taking an interest and making an effort on our behalf. If we bitch and moan about someone or some external event, it doesn't hurt to hear something empathetic, along the lines of "Well, that sounds hurtful or unfair"...you get the picture. Then, once we feel we are being *understood*, the fog which obscures reason may begin to lift and we can start to proactively pull ourselves out of it.

Please don't just throw drugs at a child and then think you've done all you can. Always question your doctors thoroughly when they offer drugs. Some antidepressants are not particularly addictive. Others are. I've been on antidepressants that were addictive and didn't know it—until I tried to get off of them and couldn't function at all.

Remember that depression usually stems from a feeling of powerlessness. The more power your Aspergirl feels within herself, the better she'll feel.

CHAPTER 17

TEMPER MELTDOWNS

Both males and females on the spectrum have temper meltdowns. While violence is less acceptable in today's society than it used to be, there is still a part of our collective psyches that sees being hot-headed as a normal part of being male. A woman who flies into a rage is merely unstable, crazy...*psycho*. If it happens in public, people would certainly think she had a psychological problem. Unless she is non-verbal and/or obviously challenged, autism would not even be considered as a possible underlying cause.

> We see girls who have trouble regulating their impulses not as having a disability, but as being non-compliant or drama queens. In other words, it is a behavior problem and discipline issue. (Stella)

I've witnessed others' temper meltdowns and thought their reaction was hyperbolic to the situation. Yet my own tantrums always seem justified. I'm sure they thought theirs were too. Why do we do it? Why can't we stop ourselves? It's not like we wake up in the morning and say "I think I'll have a meltdown today," it just happens. What sets off our rage can be multi-factorial, from a combined sensory, social, and emotional experience, such as going to a party with loud music and lots of people;

or trying to exchange a faulty product in a loud store with an uncooperative salesperson attending you. A sudden change in lifestyle or routine can also be difficult—for example when you move, are on holiday, or start a new job or relationship. These meltdowns are an outpouring of rage, and when you scratch beneath the surface of rage even a tiny bit, you find pain. Pain which builds up in cumulative, often combative, frustration.

> I feel a surge of anxiety and body sensations that build throughout the day…then they burst. These meltdowns as much as I hate to admit it are quite comparable to a tantrum that a child has in a store when he/she is told they cannot have the toy. (Brandi)

When a temper meltdown is building, the feeling is not usually as heavy as before a depression meltdown. It's more like an extreme tension; an electricity. In my case I feel angry, agitated, sometimes dizzy; I'm not breathing right. When I speak, if I can speak, I may be sarcastic and scornful. You might not even be able to tell it's coming until right before. Then clouds gather in my head, and you can see it in my eyes—Hurricane Rudy is imminent. It is unleashed very suddenly and I might have little or no control over it. A temper meltdown can mean public tears and outrage; yelling, swearing, and being vicious. We might say things we don't mean but at the time they seem true. We can be scary when we rise up, when all of that bottled anger and frustration finally finds its vent. It's destructive and chaotic. I once wrote a song called "Velvet":

> I'm so scary, call me Carrie White, you heard hell hath no fury.

This line was based on my meltdowns and how I reminded myself of the character from the Stephen King novel who could destroy with just the power of her wrath.

We are emotionally raw like children. And like children crying "not fair," one of the many things that can trigger a temper meltdown is the feeling that we are being taken *unfair* advantage of.

> During a break between classes at college, I caught a friend cheating at gin rummy. The game wasn't serious, it was to pass the time, nothing else. I had a violent meltdown, punched him, then I fainted. Others there said he never threw a punch back or tried to defend himself, he was just stunned. I remember the meltdown, but not the fight. I came out of it with an EMT (Emergency Medical Technician) standing over me. (Dame Kev)

Injustice can also start the fire burning—when we feel others are being taken advantage of. I loved vigilante films like those of Clint Eastwood and Charles Bronson when I was a kid, because I hated to see wrongdoers get away with stuff. (I've since learned about karma, or I'd probably be sporting a poncho and nunchuks today.) When I was 14, I found out my friend's father was making her have sex with him. I tried to hide her at my house but he came after her and I flipped. I wanted to kill him but I took it out on his car instead, hitting it with my bare fists. I felt no pain but afterwards I saw it was dented all over.

We are more susceptible to meltdowns when we're *hungry*. Children in supermarkets—famous example. Too many items, lights, people going by, music, chatter…and all that food. Restaurants are another likely setting.

> I can have a meltdown when I go without eating for a while. I once threatened to throw rocks at peoples heads if the line didn't "f-ing move." (Elfinia)

> I went to a taqueria and I wanted an avocado tostada and they wouldn't make it for me. I got annoyed that there was nothing there that I could eat because I am a vegetarian. I started crying in front of everyone and ended up feeling really sick and horrible for the rest

of the day. I also threw up. I will often throw up after having meltdowns. (Olive)

Having a meltdown when we're being *falsely accused* makes us look dangerous or unhinged, and merely strengthens others' negative opinion of us.

> About a year ago my son was attending a YMCA kids workshop, where a counselor suspected there may have been physical abuse to him by my hand. It seemed so horrible that the place I took him to for emotional help was having this suspicion. I was so offended at the false accusation that I lost it, becoming very verbally aggressive and abusive to the staff; I spoke in this weird sarcastic tone, which only reinforced their suspicions of me. My son was taken away by Child Protective Services to a foster home and I didn't see him for a month. I did not even realize that what I was doing would result in police and court intervention. (Ann Marie)

The more outrageous the accusation, the greater the rage meltdown will be. Unfortunately rage only implicates us, makes us look guilty to the person who does not understand Asperger syndrome.

Getting *ripped off* can be another impetus. Sales pitches that promise one thing and then deliver another; customers that refuse to pay; people who borrow something and don't return it.

> The worst temper meltdown I've had in recent years was at a woman I was doing some gardening for. She decided she only wanted to pay me half of what we agreed on, but she waited until I sweated for many hours in the hot sun before she told me. I screamed and bawled like a baby at the injustice of it. Half the neighborhood heard. (Tandy)

Social/sensory overload:

> I have tantrums when I find people stupid and annoying or when too many persons surround me and I am in a situation where I can't leave. My biggest tantrums lately have been at work at meetings. The head of the library has had special talks with me about this. I'm quite frightening at these times and there is no way of stopping me. (Siv)

Temper meltdowns may be childlike but if you are 18 years old, according to the law you are an adult and should behave like one.

> Workmen coming, going, banging around and overwhelming paint smell stinging my nose—all of this change, all of this stimulation, and none of it under my control. I felt helpless, raw. I didn't think. I just struck my dad in the face. My boyfriend called the police. They kicked open the door, and tackled me to the floor in our foyer. I panicked, the sounds and sensations in my head static, trying to find a home like a radio dial between channels. *I must not lash out. I must retain speech. If I don't the cops won't understand. Why? Why can't I stop?* That's what I keep asking myself. That's the shame, fear, anxiety, and pain…I was taken to a mental health facility and upon being deemed harmless, released. No one needs to tell me that violence is unacceptable—physical or otherwise. I know Asperger syndrome is not a get-out-of-jail-free card that exempts me from responsibility for my own actions. (Stella)

Meltdowns can be triggered by *touch*, whether painful touch, for example from dentists; but even from those who are supposed to be pampering us, like hairdressers, massage therapists, and manicurists.

Confusion can be another cause; panic, or extreme fear. I recently left my wallet at a security gate at an airport. Traveling with two emotional support dogs and a laptop, I wasn't traveling light. I got confused and left my wallet on top of the security scanner that your carry-ons have to go through. Once on the plane, checking for my wallet, I flew into a panic, pulling things out of my bag, throwing them onto the seat. I pushed my way off the plane with little regard for others' physical boundaries. I kept myself from full meltdown because of fear of airport security and being thrown off the plane. I asked my fellow passenger, once the wallet was found and returned to me and we'd settled in for our flight, what it was like to for her to observe the situation.

> I could tell something was wrong with you, but I couldn't tell what. You were all over the place, your eyes were far away. I was trying to tell you something, to talk to you, but you couldn't hear, you just kept saying "I need my wallet" over and over again. I felt helpless. (Nancy)

"Helpless" is definitely the feeling others have when witnessing a meltdown. If one is not vested in the situation (or on a plane) one can just walk away. But if you live with someone and have to deal with them on an ongoing basis it is bound to have an affect on your relationship with that person and their own mental health.

> Once she starts melting down I feel helpless; there's not a whole lot of comfort I can bring. It's scary. She is no longer accepting any sort of advice—it's like white noise. It's like trying to affect a wave, it's coming after you; what do you do? You dive underneath to avoid getting pummeled by it and then you just brace yourself for what's to come. You still want to help but you have to wait for the storm to pass. Afterwards you feel drained. (My partner, Mike)

ADVICE TO ASPERGIRLS

The day I figure out how a person with Asperger's can avoid meltdowns is the day I win the Nobel prize. But let's not assume they are inevitable. Be as scientific about your meltdowns as you are about everything else—*Cause/Solution*. Know your own triggers—make a list. Refer to it often and add to it when you discover a new one. Share this information with partners or parents.

Shopping puts us in a precarious state. Always take snacks and water, have breaks, don't try to navigate too many shops in one day. If you have a new supermarket to fathom, be sure to do it a few aisles at a time, don't try to buy a week's supply on your first trip. And don't go hungry!

While some Aspergirls I spoke to never had pre-menstrual syndrome (PMS) (also called PMT or pre-menstrual tension), others turned into a raging Medusa on a monthly basis. PMS can make us susceptible to meltdowns of either the depression or temper variety. Eating healthy helps. Avoid high sugar and salt foods and too much alcohol. There are holistic supplements for PMS, such as evening primrose oil, that help with symptoms. Birth control, while it regulates periods, can make an already sensitive Aspergirl insane, so if you decide to take it watch your state of mind. If you start feeling seriously depressed and moody, it might be the pill. Find a lower-dose pill and see if that works or talk to a good obgyn (Doctor of Obstetrics and Gynecology) for an alternative. We are products of hormones, our state of mind the result of chemicals. Do your best to harness your mood so that is doesn't take you on a Disney World-sized emotional ride.

Be aware that you are not the only one being affected by your meltdowns. It is hell for us but it is also really difficult for those around us; family and even strangers may be upset and shaken by what they see. Even though we feel like we are completely alone when it happens, we are not. Children particularly are affected and just because they seem to get "used to it," they don't—it's bound to affect them. Communicate as much as possible, explain what it is and why. Other people will feel less guilty or complicit if they realize it is a product of autism and not something they did or didn't do.

Do what you need to do for their sake and also for your own. If antidepressants help, take them; some girls go to online forums, al-anon (organization for families and friends of alcoholics), others to counselors. Do what it takes to protect your own sanity and also that of your loved ones.

ADVICE TO PARENTS

If your daughter, whether she is little or not, is having temper tantrums in supermarkets or other superstores, she has sensory overload. Too many items for her mind to process, with music playing, people going by and chattering. The first time you take her to a new store, tell her you are going to visit the first two aisles. Let her find where her favorite foods are in those aisles. Those will be markers; the next time she goes, she'll feel more at home in those aisles—she will have conquered them already and can grab the jar of peanut butter with triumph. The next time you go add two more aisles. This is not practical when you have a big shop to do, so don't do it then. Do it when you have some time to show her the ropes. If she is very little, get her some funky sunglasses to cut down the glare from the lights and bring her fave soft toy.

If your daughter is having temper meltdowns *at you*, you of course want to look for the sensory causes, hunger, etc., and then ask yourself what you are doing to upset her. Are you criticizing or instigating; making her feel guilty for being herself, blaming her for something she says she hasn't done? Pull back and remember to always use positive reinforcement with your Aspergirl. Of course I'm not suggesting you cater to whims and allow her to manipulate you with tantrums. She has to learn there are consequences to losing her temper, and if you take away a privilege when she does, she'll learn. But start while she's young—it won't do any good to threaten her with not seeing *SpongeBob SquarePants* if she's in her twenties. And when she's young she's more receptive and her character is developing.

I once heard an elderly English lady say "Manners are the oil that make society run smoothly." It's a good rule to follow, autistic or not, but the visual aspect of it is something we can latch onto.

As with depression meltdowns and stimming, an outlet for her energy and a soothing quiet environment when she needs it are essential. Drugs are a last resort.

18

BURNING BRIDGES

I burn bridges. That was a side effect of being undiagnosed and unaware of Asperger syndrome. When things didn't work out on a job, or with a friend, with a city or even with a country, I would leave it. As I said earlier, for a while I developed a mindset of *there's something wrong with the world, it isn't me,* and that made it not only easy to leave flawed situations behind, but imperative. This is not always a bad thing. Some places and people are bad for you. Some situations are more progressive, healthier for mind and spirit. But when you've circumnavigated the globe twice, are middle-aged and are still burning bridges, it's perhaps time to take stock and see what's what. Figuring out I had Asperger's made me want to dig my heels in and deal with every situation, but of course, that's not good either. I had and still have to learn what to keep and what to throw in the goodwill bin.

Burning bridges and starting again is such a defining feature of my life I thought that I'd ask other Aspergirls if they do the same and all but one said that was a defining characteristic of hers as well.

When things get so bad I can't take it anymore, I up and leave, burning every bridge behind me. The phoenix is a personal symbol of mine for that reason. Burn it all and rise from the ashes. (Bramble)

This shows up in the Diagnostic and Statistical Manual of Mental Disorders (DSM) criteria as subtext, neatly hidden inside "failure to develop peer relationships"—we do develop them briefly, but then we toss them away.

> I feel like I am getting revenge when I burn a bridge. I think "that person will be really lost without me; they took me for granted and did not realize how much I helped them." (Ann Marie)

Burning bridges is a sort of psychic pyromania. We get angry at somebody or some thing, and we want to let them know that we don't need them anymore—that we never really did need them. When we burn a bridge, we are saying that we are the ones with power over our lives. The trouble with this is that it is usually done in the heat of the moment. When we are more cool-headed, we realize that we still want to shop at that store, or we still want to see that friend, or we do need that job after all. Like pyromania, it feels good at the time, empowering, but it is usually irreversibly destructive.

Burning bridges is often the result of depression meltdowns. The clouds won't lift so we seek new horizons, a new stage on which to perform our play.

> I get depressed, get very low, kick out at everything and everyone. Hate my life, hate myself, hate the people around me. I get out of it by changing as much around me as possible—quit a job, leave a relationship, sell my house, etc. (Sam)

It is often the end result of temper meltdowns. We get very angry at a place, person, or thing and resolve never to deal with them again. Sometimes, after a temper meltdown, we can't—because we are banished outright or our embarrassment is too great to revisit the situation. Burning bridges is triggered by many of the same things; it's the last straw of being misunderstood—we get sick and tired of people not getting us, taking us for granted; not showing us the love and appreciation we feel we deserve. We don't learn from our mistakes as easily as others, partly because we have memory problems. We often may not remember why we got angry at someone. We might forgive and forget until it happens again and again…instead of protecting ourselves all along, we remain vulnerable and then blow up, once and for all severing a connection.

> If I don't like a situation it's so much easier to just walk away, avoid it and never look back. Usually it's just a relief but then if I'm avoiding someone I have to worry about running into them so it can add some stress too. I have a really bad memory so after some time has passed, if I run into someone, I'm just like nothing ever happened. (Nikki)

Burning bridges affects our family lives—we may leave husbands or parents; siblings; friends that let us down; people who we feel have used us. This causes us to pour the proverbial kerosene and strike the match.

> It seems to happen quite a bit. Mostly when the empathy give and take shuts down. (Dame Kev)

Burning bridges is triggered by injustice—we do not want to patronize or support any ideology, institution, or person that goes against our strongly held ethics and views. Burning bridges affects employment. We have bad experiences on the job, so often, particularly when we're younger, we will leave a job abruptly without giving notice.

> I am definitely a bridge burner! I could probably have stood to give my two weeks notice at the last couple of

jobs. I left with no notice and that made it extremely hard to find that next job. (Elfinia)

As a person of a certain age who has had the benefit of seeing history repeat itself in my life, over and over again, I can see that burning bridges is, for lack of a better phrase, bad karma. When I blow up a bridge to a place or element of my past, I merely stumble upon a similar village a little further down the road. The climate may be different, the language also, but the story will play out very similarly.

As an Asperger's consultant, I often hear people with AS who are fed up with their life experience put the blame solely on others. They think that they can change their luck by changing jobs, towns, etc. Sometimes you can, and while you should always seek out your ideal environment, at the same time, if you are leaving in haste and bitterness, be warned, history will repeat itself for you too. You have to leave a situation mindfully and as graciously as you possibly can. If you don't believe in karma, I'm sure you can at least believe in *references* and *recommendations*—by behaving this way, you will have none of those. It can also affect your reputation and make it harder for people to entrust you with their friendship.

Burning bridges is closely related to the *pre-emptive strike* which many of us are also good at—quit before you are fired, dump them before they dump you, leave before things get messy. We do develop a tendency to sense trouble ahead. We learn to read the signs the way cats feel earthquakes coming and birds know winter is on its way. Cynics may call it a self-fulfilling prophecy.

Sometimes our bridges get burnt for us when our meltdowns get particularly bad. I have read that females with Asperger's tend to be a little more prone to physical temper tantrums than their male counterparts. I would say, based on observation and interviews, this might be true. I'm not entirely sure that males burn bridges as well. I don't think that they do it as often. I believe, based on my own experience, that it does sometimes coincide with PMS; enough to see a correlation. As our bodies are cleaning house, so do our psyches. PMS makes us more temperamental, more apt to say things, not necessarily that we don't mean, but that we might not say at other times.

> I need to clean house a lot, metaphorically speaking, to cope, to keep the clutter in my personal life down. (Anemone)

I believe also that this tendency of self-imposed change may throw doctors off the Asperger's scent. We normally do not like change. For example, we hate it when our supermarket gets torn down and a new one put up, because we have to re-map it and re-learn what triggers will be lurking there. Burning a bridge, on the other hand, is something in our control. It's our way of saying we don't need a store at *all*. Of course sometimes we are not right, and we can regret it later.

> My life is a series of burned bridges. At the time, it feels as if I am *right* and that I am standing up for what I believe in. Often I am. I have, however, learned in the past decade that I can be very black and white in my thinking. (Camilla)

ADVICE TO ASPERGIRLS

Sometimes, in the throes of a meltdown particularly, we cannot see *any other perspective* but our own and this reflects what I've been trying to say about our lens. It is often about *how* we are looking at something in the moment, not what we are looking at. Now I know that as a person with AS, you have probably been gossiped about, bullied, taken advantage of and it has built up and built up and then finally, like steam, it finds its vent. That is why it is so important to learn how to stand up for yourself tactfully and with strength as you go through your life.

Most of the people and situations you will encounter in your life will have a mix of attributes, and as stated earlier, it is about resonating with and bringing out the higher qualities of those people and situations. We get blind-sided. We have bad memories. People can fool us and hurt us over and over again, till we get fed up. One trick you can try to avoid disillusionment, to avoid being blind-sided, is to have a list of traits you need to remind yourself of, every time you see a person—for example: "This is Sally, she's my co-worker. She's a nice person but she doesn't always tell the truth. Therefore, don't believe everything she says." That way you are on your guard and you are not shocked and horrified when she lies to you for the umpteenth time and you figure it out too late.

You can do the same thing with places. "This is Best Buy. It is a big, loud store. I need to eat before I go and bring water, earplugs, and sunglasses or a hat with a visor. Some of the salespeople are helpful, some are not. I will remain calm and only speak to those who seem happy to assist me."

If you do leave a situation, it is important to try to leave things with people, jobs, etcetera on the best terms possible so that your conscience is clear, so your new start is a fresh one, and there won't be any guilt or other ties pulling you back into the old situation.

Remember the three Rs: references, recommendations, reputation. You may need all three at some point, untarnished, to get what you want.

ADVICE TO PARENTS

Watch for the warning signs that a bridge is about to be burnt. Mainly they comprise excuses, apathy, criticisms, and complaints. If she needs a little incentive to get through college or stay in a job, try to find something. It may be more valuable to just sit down with her and find out the source of angst or dissatisfaction and see if there's anything that can be done about it.

What if it is you she wants to burn the bridge to? You'd have to start by asking yourself why—why would your daughter want to leave you behind? What did you do that was so terrible? To again refer to M.J. Carley's book (2008), many of us will be angry at our parents for not recognizing that we were different and had special needs. Carley says it is important that we forgive our parents, because they probably weren't bad parents, they were just normal people and had no frame of reference at the time for understanding. Talk to her about this. Apologize if necessary.

Children only want to be loved by their parents, no matter what their age. It means a lot to me that my mom, at the age of 73, has begun to turn the television sound off when I visit, instead of shouting things at me over the commercials. If you and your daughter are younger than me and my mom, I'd suggest you make a real effort to get to know her; her likes and dislikes, and what she wants and needs from you. It will not be good for either of you to be estranged from one another.

19

STOMACH ISSUES AND AUTISM

Look at most autism trait lists and you will find "stomach and intestinal problems." One almost feels led to believe that autism somehow causes stomach problems. Most of the world's top autism researchers and doctors now believe that it is the other way around—autism is initially caused by a compromised digestive system which allows toxins from the environment and food to get into the bloodstream and impact brain development at crucial stages. The popular autism diets—the gluten-free, casein-free diet (GFCF) and specific carbohydrate diet (SCD) also operate on the premise of a compromised intestinal tract. A "leaky gut" doesn't allow proper processing of elements found in milk and wheat (as well as some other grains). These elements become toxic and impede brain development and functioning.

Donna Gates, author of *The Body Ecology Diet* (2006) and Dr. Natasha Campbell-McBride, author of *Gut and Psychology Syndrome* (2004) both also say, very convincingly, that autism is caused by the lack of healthy digestive flora in the body. Things like poor diet (with too many processed foods and not enough fermented foods), too many antibiotics, not being breastfed, these all impact a woman's flora which she then passes on to her child.

If Donna, Natasha, and others are right, then it stands to reason: most, if not *all*, people with Asperger's and autism will have some form of digestive issue. Gastro-intestinal (GI) problems make themselves apparent—you don't have to be a doctor to know if you have chronic irritable bowel syndrome (IBS) or heartburn. I looked at my own situation first: my mother came of age in the 1950s and her diet from that point on consisted largely of processed and canned foods—Wonder Bread, Campbell's Soup and other great American staples. She had severe, bleeding ulcers when I was a young child and I was diagnosed with a duodenal ulcer at age 12, followed by a lifetime of IBS. I had assumed that was due to severe bullying and anxiety. But perhaps there was more to it than that. So I asked others on the spectrum. Researching for another book (Simone 2010) I found that 9 out of 10 did have problems *that they knew of.* For this book, all but two had significant stomach and intestinal issues that they are aware of, from IBS to ulcers to food allergies. Here is a partial list of what the Aspergirls have that are directly related to digestion or that may be related:

> Chronic nausea, mild to severe food allergies (mostly wheat, dairy), migraines, guttate psoriasis, hypothyroidism, "malaise and fogginess from eating processed food," irritable bowel syndrome (IBS), hiatal hernia, constipation, ulcers, heartburn; sensitive, irritated skin; chronic fatigue syndrome, fibromyalgia, food feels like glass in stomach, diagnosed leaky gut, strong sugar and salt cravings, complete lack of appetite, no interest in food.

Some of these experiences occurred daily, with high levels of pain, but the Aspergirls, myself included, had them so long that we'd come to accept them as a fact of life. Many of us were aware that our mothers also had GI issues. While this doesn't prove anything, it enforces the theory of the autism–gut connection.

Gates, Campbell-McBride, and others, say that the cure as well as the cause of autism is already here: it lies in food. The diets they promote are very restrictive—Gates' Body Ecology

Diet, for example, involves drinking something called "young coconut kefir." Because of taste, habit, budget, and time, most of us will never try these diets even if we had absolute proof that they worked, and so far that has largely been anecdotal.

But it seems obvious that if autism truly starts in the gut, and you heal the gut, you should see an improvement in symptoms. When we are older, our brains are already developed, but like any organ, still very much affected by what we put into our bodies. I knew my task wouldn't be easy but I wanted to find out if we could improve our stomach health with the aim of seeing if it improved AS symptoms. But how do you get busy grownup Aspergirls, with jobs, kids, and college classes, to disrupt their routine? Was there an easier way than to go on a strict diet? Merely by chance I heard of a product called Amrit that was purported to be the most powerful antioxidant in the world, with claims of a very positive impact on *digestive* problems. It also claimed to improve health of mind, brain, and nerves; increase vitality and inner strength; enhance coordination of mental and physical functions, and more—all things which seem relevant and useful to an autistic. The company, MAPI, generously donated a two months' supply to 12 of us. I gave the supplements—Amrit Nectar and Amrit Ambrosia—to the women on condition that they keep a journal of stomach health, moods/anxiety levels, and meltdowns. I also asked some of the Aspergirls to keep records of what they ate for two weeks, and found that none of them were on "autism-friendly" diets. In fact, while there were many fresh fruits and vegetables consumed, there were also lots of high salt, high sugar, processed, packaged foods on top of that.

What I found interesting is that some of the girls I offered the Amrit to refused to try it on the grounds that they either didn't believe ASDs could be cured or aided by improved digestion, or else they didn't *want* to be cured. Further, some of the Aspergirls with the worst symptoms—high anxiety levels, frequent, severe meltdowns, rampant sensory issues, were most likely to reject it:

on the grounds that they didn't want to introduce anything new into their bodies or routines.

What I found when I took the supplement and what the participating Aspergirls found was an almost immediate evening out of mood, with a noticeable cessation of anxiety. Some of us got a slightly euphoric feeling, as if we'd taken an antidepressant. While it started out well, in a very short time most of us began to suffer digestive problems which ranged from glass-like pain and constipation, to diarrhea and hemorrhoids. At this point two girls threw their tablets away or returned them to me. One dropped out without further contact.

Autistic people need lower doses of drugs and supplements as our bodies are too sensitive. Some cannot even take a multivitamin without becoming sick. The remaining participants decreased our dose from two of each tablet, to less than one each per day. The company added another natural product to ease the digestion problems and it worked. We were soon able to take the supplements without those side effects. The trial lasted two months. Those who stuck with it felt more even keel, had a decrease in the number and nature of mood swings and meltdowns. Some experienced a decrease in anxiety with a decrease in the need to stim. Some could handle social situations and interactions a little better. This was not a scientific, clinically controlled study and I do not purport it as such, but I do think the results were positive. Why is this worth mentioning?

Because, first, if autism truly does start with the gut it is only logical that if you heal the gut you improve autistic symptoms. Second, the amount of daily pain and poor health that I and others have had to endure is something that we've come to accept—but the reality is, it should be unacceptable.

ADVICE TO ASPERGIRLS

Try to clean up your diet of any artificial, chemical, processed food, and additives, and get your body used to a healthy, non-toxic intake. That might pave the way to trying something a bit more on the dramatic side. I can't see going from a diet of Ho-hos and Hot Pockets to the Body Ecology Diet, but I can see making a segue from an organic, mostly plant-based, whole food diet to that.

> I have discovered that if I increase my exercise level and liver cleanse that I feel fantastic and weight, pain, and emotional issues are less of a problem. (Tina)

Many of us believe that we would be lesser people without Asperger's—take away autism completely and you take away genius. I am not peddling a cure. However, if you are not digesting properly you are not getting the most nourishment from your food. If you have stomach problems, you've probably had them so long that you've come to accept either the pain or the Rolaids chaser after every meal as a fact of life. Those symptoms listed above *are not our natural state!* Nature did not intend for you to be in pain every day of your life. Nor did it intend for you to eat food from a can or a tube. Most people in America and other western countries don't even know what real foods taste like, they only know when extreme amounts of sugar or salt or other things hit their mouth and their bloodstream and this problem has spread throughout the globe, along with the autism epidemic. Be your own body detective, investigate diets, supplements, eat as humans were intended to eat and start from there to decide which particular path you want to take to achieve *complete gastro-intestinal health.* It *can* be yours if you want it.

ADVICE TO PARENTS

Start her on a special diet when she's young, while her brain is still developing; while you still have control over what she eats. Many Aspergirls have an addiction to sugar, which is not good for intestinal flora, and processed foods should be completely avoided. The diets mentioned will involve a lifestyle change and should be undertaken while tastes and habits are more easily formed. Don't assume there is nothing you can do about your daughter's IBS and other health issues. There is a cause for *everything*. It stands to reason that if you eliminate the cause, you eliminate or improve the condition.

20

Getting Older on the Spectrum

Getting older, like autism itself, is something of a victim of bad press. While some of the disadvantages of getting older are magnified for spectrum gals, so are some of the benefits. Since many women aren't diagnosed until they are middle-aged, there can be a real settling into the diagnosis and feeling "at home" in your skin for the very first time. We still have the same reactions to things but now we know the all-important *why*. Add to that the self-knowledge and awareness that comes with age and you can understand that many of us will be happier in our forties and fifties than we ever were before.

> I think aging is the best kept secret. Everyone talks it up as something terrible—but I love it! I love menopause, I love my silvering hair, I love my senior citizen discount. I am less hyper and less self-centered. I am letting go of baggage. I may be figuring out things that NTs have down by thirty, but I am pleased as heck with my current level of wisdom, and look forward to its continuing development. (Widders)

Since a substantial number of Aspergirls don't like sex and a large number don't want babies, menopause may actually be a welcome end to inconvenient cycles and hormones. Old age brings a bit of androgyny to everyone. Since femininity isn't one of our goals, many won't care about seeming less feminine and attractive to the opposite sex. We take a pragmatic approach to our appearance. Some of us will be fascinated by the scientific processes of aging and will even welcome them.

> I do remember the moment when I realized I was no longer attractive. It gave me some relief, actually. (Widders)

It's not too easy to find diagnosed grandmothers to talk to (I found only two), but it seems that they really enjoy the role of Aspergranny. Where a more conventional grandparent might be more about buying presents, we are more likely to get down on the floor with the kiddies and play. We have had to live through seeing our children—our playmates—grow up, and that is sad for us. Having grandkids means a whole new set of playmates.

> I have five children and four grandchildren. Most are on the spectrum. I love to engage with small people, live alongside them as they grow, learn and mature. (Pokégran)

Less tolerance for stress also comes with age, but even that has its positive side. Since our anxiety levels have always been very high, and our nerves have been a taut thread pretty much forever, we will now find we have to do something about it or the thread will snap. That means clearly defining to ourselves and others, our needs and our boundaries. For example it may have been fairly easy for Type A personalities to take advantage of us, for those that can prey on the socially weak often will (Type A personalities can be described as ambitious, aggressive, assertive, and combative). One of the massive benefits I'm finding that comes with age is that I can see through that behavior so clearly now and while on some level I always could, now I am no longer afraid to say "no" and put a stop to it. I may have reached a level in this regard that most women would reach in their teens and twenties, but at least it's been reached.

> I have some regrets that make more sense because I know of Asperger's now. This sometimes relieves me, and sometimes makes me sad that I did not know about my AS sooner. Even though I'm now in a relationship (two years), I don't know if it can last because of my AS, and I sometimes think I may end up alone like my mom did for the last twenty years of her life. Sometimes I think this would be terrible, and sometimes I like the idea of being alone as I get older. (Ann Marie)

Another trait of getting older is that we get tired of hiding our quirks and our sensitivities. Many Aspergirls tell me that people in their lives, doctors, employers, family members, etc., expect them to get more "normal" as they get older, more able to deal with certain aspects of life. But what is more likely to happen for us is that we get more quirky and more eccentric; we don't ever seem to assimilate into the mainstream. That is why so many older folks are getting diagnosed—we're fed up with pretending because we just can't keep it up any longer.

> What most practitioners don't know is that I am slowly declining in my ability to function. (Brandi)

The biggest problems for women getting older on the spectrum are:

- poverty
- loneliness
- health issues.

Poverty is a major issue for us because of unemployment, underemployment, or not getting a living wage. There aren't too many services for adults on the high-functioning end of the spectrum apart from social groups. That's well and fine, but it doesn't help us pay the bills. With the DSM changing the Asperger diagnosis (at time of writing, we are not certain of its exact wording or nature) it is my hope that adults with Asperger's will be able to get some laws protecting them as well as easier access to public assistance or other programs for those with disabilities. There's so much stigma around disabilities, and, because Aspergirls are highly functional in some ways, people look at us and think "there's nothing wrong with you, go get a job." As I hope I've illustrated in this book and in Simone 2010, there are so many issues at play, sometimes we simply can't work with others. We need jobs that work with our strengths, and our intelligence. We need special job coaches, with AS-specific training.

Britain has just passed the Autism Act—as usual our socially democratic cousins across the pond are one step ahead of us. While US departments are always downsizing help programs, the Brits understand that stigmatizing a person does little for self-esteem and motivation. A country that kicks its meek is headed down a slippery slope (and isn't half as Christian as it pretends to be).

Many of us will have to work under whatever circumstances are offered and we'll be fish out of water for most of our lives. No matter what our age, we must start now, creating the right livelihood for our social, sensory and cognitive issues. This is of particular importance for those of us with no partners and no one to help take care of us as we get older.

> If I could retire (I *hate* working) with enough to eat and have a place with my dogs, life would be truly grand. (Widders)

Loneliness: While many isolated Aspergirls are okay with being alone, many are not, and it is much more difficult to meet new people when you are older, eccentric, and have no money to get out and about. Our children/playmates have grown and gone. Many of us will have had husbands who we married for the wrong reasons or pre-diagnosis and those husbands may have left us for our unusual behavior.

Unlike men, women can't/don't/won't go to the usual places men might go to meet others, such as a club, bar, etc., on their own. This is true when we're younger for fear of looking like we're on the prowl. But when you're middle-aged or older, you can look desperate. (Not *my* rules.) An Aspergirl with her aversion to socializing has a doubly difficult time.

If we never received social skills training and have had many poor relationships with people—friendships that soured, etc.—we may get worse at socializing rather than better, and more reclusive than ever.

Health issues: The stresses and strains of Asperger's, including PTSD, no health insurance; being unable to afford basic necessities like dental work, good food, decent, warm clothes; a safe and quiet environment, along with depression, are more tolerable when you're young, but have a cumulative and debilitating effect. By a certain age, they become a crisis.

A combination of poverty and health crises might mean ending up in a nursing home. Shared housing of any kind can be very difficult for an Aspergirl—growing old in a nursing home, with all the noises and smells and different personalities that don't know what your triggers are and don't care, could be a potential nightmare. People with AS should have their own room in such a situation and nursing home staff should be trained about AS...one informed person can make all the difference.

ADVICE TO ASPERGIRLS

It is possible to grow old with grace, dignity, style, and flair. And as stated we finally begin to come into our own in so many wonderful ways.

Take good care of your health starting now because you will only get more vulnerable as you get older.

Do avoid the tendency to become a total recluse. I hold in my mind the picture of a grumpy old woman that all the neighborhood kids are scared or make fun of, and it makes me try a little harder! Picture the kind of person you'd like to be, and don't be afraid to share your insights and gifts with others.

Weigh the pros and cons of a relationship if you don't have one yet…wouldn't it be nice to have someone to grow old with, to rely on? And gender issues take on less meaning for us as we get older. The male/female roles that may have put you off when you were younger, aren't so important in your 40s and up.

Start looking at ways to dramatically increase your income if you haven't already. You'll want and need a specific sort of environment with control over it as you get older.

21

ON WHETHER ASPERGER SYNDROME IS A DISABILITY OR A GIFT, AND ADVICE FROM ASPERGIRLS TO ASPERGIRLS

In order to determine whether AS is a disability or a gift, I have to ask myself if I am truly disabled. Of course I prefer differently-abled. We are overly-abled in some areas, super-enabled even. We can read books and understand anything written better than most, but can't follow social conversation. We can dismantle computers and install hardware, but we can't find our way around a supermarket. We can monologue for ages on our special interests, but can't spend an hour in conversation without getting a migraine or having a meltdown. We can paint pictures and design things of astonishing beauty, but can't be bothered to fix our own hair. We can write novels, but can't make an imaginative supper.

Some people think that AS only exists in relation to others, that if everyone were on the spectrum they wouldn't feel disabled. I agree that I'd feel less odd, but I'd still have many sensory issues, and I have a hard time listening to other Aspies monologuing without getting brain-strain. I have also hurt the feelings of others on the spectrum because they, like me, are very sensitive and I'm blunt.

Many now agree that if you remove the autism, you remove the gifts. While of course we don't want to see people suffer with extreme autism, the thought of eradicating it through things like genetic selection is sad and frightening. While there have been many times I've wished I'd never been born, it is annoying and insulting when well-meaning people say "I'm sorry" when I tell them I have Asperger's. If it weren't for Asperger's and obsessions there would be no Theory of Relativity, no *Magic Flute*, no Microsoft…and no *Ghost Busters*. Here's what the Aspergirls had to say about having Asperger's.

> I'm a lucky person in this respect, because I have a measured and recorded very high IQ and have made a career as a specialist. This has also made me good at passing as a person without difficulties to the outside world. People close to me, like my ex-partners and my son, know that I have great disabilities in taking care of myself and my home, for example. But nevertheless, I would never ever want to change or be more "normal." I get so much out of my special interests, my collections, and am easily stimulated and satisfied in most ways of life. I see AS more like a large part of my personality, and I can't think of myself without it. (Siv)

> Even the social isolation has benefits, in that one can be free of the dominant thought to see things uniquely. (Widders)

> When it comes to educational pursuits and intellectual ability, I think AS is a wonderful gift. I can hyperfocus. I like tedious tasks. I adore logical problem solving. My brain might hold the technology of the future. However, when I look at my life and realize I've never been in a real relationship, I can't attend most social events, I'm the

easiest person to take advantage of, and the populated world in general completely overwhelms me, I realize I'm not like other people. The funny thing is, if the rest of the world was just like me I don't think I'd feel disabled at all. (Andi)

I have gifts—a great mind, insights, the capacity to paint and draw. It is also a disability. I cannot work with others without conflict and worry, confusion and exhaustion. (Camilla)

Over the years I've noticed, as I became more "normal"/less visibly autistic, I have much less focus than I did. I suspect that my visual memory is less sharp because I rely on and practice language more often than my first language. Get rid of the disability and you also get rid of the gift. (Stella)

When I read about the possibility of determining what causes AS, I experience concern that there is an imperative to change it. In my mind determining the cause is only useful for knowing whether a person has it and then offering that person every opportunity to be valued for their own specific "diamonds" and assisting them with the "shit." As far as changing it, forget it…as hard and painful as my life has been, I would not want to be normal. (Tina)

It's important to realize that how much AS is a disability depends on everyone else and how inclusive they feel like being. (Anemone)

I know others see it as a gift, and have real gifts because of it—savant skills, amazing talents born of special interests, amazing ability to visualize or design or hyperfocus. But I don't have any of those, and for me, AS is a disability. In the Aspie Rights area, there's the growing ideology that AS people be allowed to just live and not be cured and not have prenatal testing trying to weed out AS from the gene pool. I don't know how I feel about that… I don't like the idea that if a parent knew they were going to have a child like me, they'd abort, but at the same time I don't know I'd wish the life I've had on that child anyway. (Polly)

I see it in the same light as astigmatism. People with astigmatism need glasses to see properly. People with AS need different tools so we "see properly" in a world full of people without AS. (Dame Kev)

In this day and age, due to the social demands of society (being flexible, being outgoing and assertive, etc.), AS will usually be seen as a disability. Perhaps in a different day and age where our other traits (such as dependability, able to do repetitive things all day, being alone) would be much more valued, then it would have been considered a gift. (Elle)

I think Aspies have always contributed to society in their way. (Jayne)

ADVICE FROM
ASPERGIRLS TO ASPERGIRLS

I asked the Aspergirls what advice they'd give to others. This list is the result:

- Get a diagnosis.

- Be proud to be different.

- Study and work in your field of interests, and AS will not stand in your way.

- Cultivate your talents and try to turn them into a marketable skill.

- Be yourself. That way you'll be found and liked by all the other people like you.

- You can be happy with Asperger's or miserable with Asperger's. I've tried both. I prefer happy.

- Autism gives us perseverance, not just to become enthralled with special interests, but to *succeed in life.*

- If you are having a crummy day, check out a chat room. You might feel alone but you are far from it.

- You have Asperger's, Asperger's doesn't have you.

- Choose men very carefully.

- Find a companion who is truly unconditional.

- Revel in solitude.

- Don't worry about what others think. It's just between you and your best self. Success is closing that gap.

- Listen to other people's observations. If they tell you they have doubts about a person or situation, they're probably right. It's a bad idea to trust intuition you don't have, and it can get you seriously hurt.

- Find ASD women mentors.

- Don't worry too much, there's usually no need.

- Be as tolerant and understanding of others as you can.

- Learn assertiveness techniques.

- Simplify life.

- Life is not about being someone else's perfect anything.

- Don't be worried about social stigma. Fight false media messages that autism means being less of a person.

- Get fit, exercise regularly, and eat carefully.

- If you feel too uncomfortable conforming to a role, change your role.

- Read a lot, not just about Asperger's.

- Don't care so much about what people in school think of you. You'll never see them again in your life after you graduate.

My advice is, be vulnerable *and* courageous. Just as eye contact contains too much information, "life contact" seems to as well. AS disables us when our extreme sensitivity becomes inverted, ingrown and morphs into a shell of protectiveness and exclusion. A burgeoning cultural awareness is happening with the arrival of films, books and news stories about Asperger's. Tell your own story.

ADDITIONAL TOOLS FOR PARENTS

CHAPTER *22*

GIVE YOUR ASPERGIRL SOME BALLS: BELIEF, ACCEPTANCE, LOVE, LIKE, AND SUPPORT

Most of the information in this book is aimed directly at Aspergirls. I'd suggest moms and dads re-read all the "Advice for parents" sections on a regular basis because you will be challenged throughout your lifetime and you will forget things that you learned, to make room for more as the years go by.

I'm a fan of things that are easy to remember, so I've come up with this handy dandy acronym, which reiterates some key points even without explanation. It sums up what I've been trying to tell you throughout the book.

The best thing you can give your Aspergirl is some BALLS: Belief, Acceptance, Love, Like, and Support.

BELIEF

Because AS is classed as a disability many people put more emphasis on the *can't* than the *can*. Inherent in having Asperger's is a lot of self-doubt and confusion so you need to bestow within your child a sense of belief that she can be anything or do anything that she wants. Believe in her dreams, her goals, her opinions, and in her intelligence. If you believe her and believe in her, then she leaves your house and enters the world with a much more solid platform than she would otherwise.

Also, if she is older and is just now diagnosed or is self-diagnosed, you might not initially believe it possible that she has Asperger's. Don't waste time and energy trying to make her doubt the diagnosis. Let the verdict settle and then read all you can.

While parents may be willing to believe the diagnosis, often other family or community members may shake their head in disbelief and refuse to accept that she is autistic. They think that autism is an "either/or" situation. Educate everyone. She doesn't need the job of convincing people on top of everything else.

If she is self-diagnosed, while you should encourage and attempt to get an official opinion, treat the prospect seriously. When an Aspergirl first realizes she has AS, she has a true Eureka! moment. Following that, she will have months, perhaps years, of learning to accept AS and what it means to her. Your rebuttal of her self-diagnosis is going to do no good whatsoever unless you have firm proof or evidence to the contrary.

ACCEPTANCE

You must accept and acknowledge the impact of Asperger's on her life. If she tells you she can't handle studying, working, or living or whatever under certain conditions, those limitations should and must be respected. She's not doing or saying it for attention or special concessions, she's reaching out for understanding. While pushing boundaries is important, small supported steps are much more effective than being thrown in the deep end.

Those at the highest-functioning end of the spectrum, while less affected, still have autism. You must accept that. For those of you who have had success with diet and other means getting your child's autism "downgraded" to Asperger's, you still have to educate yourself about AS and accept the challenges that come with that situation.

Accept that she has Asperger's. Accept her for who she is. This will minimize the chance of comorbid psychological conditions and increase her chances for positive self-esteem.

LOVE

Obviously if you as a parent don't love her, then there's going to be a part of her that will always feel like she doesn't deserve to be loved—basic psychology. Of course you probably do love your daughter. Yet, how many of us follow the words with "I love you, *but…*" This kind of talk says that love is conditional; that we would love them more if they were less *this* or more *that*. You must love her. For if you do not, what sort of hope has she got in this world? She will be looking for something to fill that emptiness. It might be an activity, it might be drugs, most likely it will be a man (or woman) to fill the void. Finding love is hard enough when you have autism, much more so when you have never had it at home and really don't know what it is. While this is important for boys I believe the consequences for girls are potentially dire. Many Aspergirls said they had been in abusive relationships early in their dating lives. Many of us have lost our virginity in inappropriate and unsatisfying ways because we did not value ourselves. Many of us have married the wrong man because we did not know what love was; what it felt like to be loved. If we aren't loved by our parents we are very likely to partner with someone who carries on the tradition our parents started.

LIKE

To like someone is more important than to love them. When you like your daughter you let her know that she's likeable, and we with AS have a hard time with that. We're not socially accepted, and we have all these issues that make us difficult to deal with sometimes. How many of us love someone in our family but do not like them? You must find a way to understand your Aspergirl, to see things from her point of view. Without that understanding and perspective, you will never know her and if you don't know her, how could you possibly like her? She will have a hard time making and keeping friends. It will be so much easier for her if she believes and knows that she is likeable; that it is a question of finding the right playmates as opposed to changing herself to fit in. Do not try to make her. Aspergirls get told by everyone from parents to job coaches that they should "fake it" to fit in. Imagine going your whole life faking your personality. Who could keep that up for long?

One of the difficulties a parent may have truly liking their daughter, might stem from the fact that because she is not demonstrative, the parent may feel that she doesn't like them.

> When she was younger, I felt as though she didn't like me. She was not affectionate, stiffened if I tried to hug her and turned her cheek if I tried to kiss her. She hated to do things that I enjoyed doing, like shopping, small talk, being with friends or family. With time and education, I learned not to take offense over these things. I have had to learn how to talk to her in a way that was not offensive to her. She would take everything we said very literally, and would often say things that were very random. I think most moms think of their daughters as extensions of themselves. It took time to learn and understood that she is not me. (Deborah)

SUPPORT

It is possible and likely that an Aspergirl will take longer to leave your house. The bird will fly the nest eventually, but if you push her out too soon you do so at her peril. She may seem mature for her age when she's little but when she is older, she will be emotionally more vulnerable than her peers. She doesn't learn from her mistakes as readily. She will be naïve romantically. She may have a difficult time finding and keeping employment. She can and she will, with help and effort, be successful at all those things but it may take a bit more time.

Her health may suffer from a lifetime of PTSD, poverty (with resultant stress and poor diet), depression from loneliness, GI issues, etc., so you can see how absolutely crucial it is not to shove her out into the world and expect the same progress from her as from non-Aspergian girls.

> With a nonautistic child you can expect certain milestones to occur in their lives on a fairly straightforward timeline. With an autistic child, you take each milestone when the child is able to get there. With a nonautistic child, you can allow her more freedom when she demonstrates she is mature enough to handle it, the whole *roots and wings* thing. An autistic child will not be able to defend herself against the unscripted, multi-faceted world that awaits her outside of her home until older. If the wings come, it won't be until much later. (Deborah)

We need support—moral, emotional, and sometimes financial support. Many Aspergirls have a hard time supporting themselves, so she might be coming to you for money or she may still live at home, and I know that's hard for you too. But we often have nowhere else to turn; government welfare and disability agencies are largely clueless. In New York state, if I wanted help I'd have to go to the Office of Mental Retardation! Since people with Asperger's have a higher-than-average IQ, and being mentally retarded connotes an IQ of 70 or less, we will be turned away at the door. There's a lot of misunderstanding and stigma attached to Asperger's because of lack of awareness. With nowhere else to turn, we often have to rely on our loved ones. If we do not have a partner, that can mean parents; even elderly ones.

The less stigmatized we feel, the more confident we feel, and that translates into the ability and wherewithal to seek employment and assume our place in the world at large.

23

THOUGHTS AND ADVICE FROM PARENTS OF ASPERGIRLS

I'm not the parent of an Aspergirl. For this chapter I enlisted the aid of Deborah Tedone, Director of Square Pegs/Asperger's Support Group for Adults in Rochester, NY. Deborah says so eloquently what all parents of AS girls need to hear.

WHAT IS THE BEST PART ABOUT BEING THE PARENT OF AN AS GIRL?

The best part about being the parent of an AS girl is that God loved me enough to entrust such a sweet, beautiful, unique being into my care. I think what I love most about being her parent is that I truly love her honesty, her brilliance (and I'm not exaggerating), her innocence, and her fierce determination to beat this world despite *its* imperfection. I respect her. I trust her. I thank God every day for her!

WHAT ARE THE BIGGEST CHALLENGES?

There are many, but not because of her, necessarily, but because of the world. When she was very young, the temper tantrums were very challenging. We didn't know what to do to help her.

She couldn't communicate to us what was wrong. She would also do things that were not age appropriate, such as demanding to wear two different shoes to school at the same time, when in Junior High. It hurts to see her not treated well by others. It tears my heart apart when I hear others picking on her or calling her names. Other people's ignorance and self-centeredness can make me very, very angry. I have spent many tears praying for people to be less cruel to her. So, so many examples. The first time was when she was three, she was sitting in the sand box in our back yard. She liked the feeling of the cool sand on her legs on hot days. When I went inside to answer the phone, I went back outside (maybe 4–5 minutes later) to find the neighbor-boy pouring buckets of sand over her head, and laughing, calling her a retard while he did it. She just sat there with her thumb in her mouth, blankly staring. When she was 17, we stood in line at a grocery store she worked at a few hours a week. The cashier didn't see us in her line, but she was talking about my daughter to the cashier in the next aisle, loud enough for us to hear. Things like, "What planet did (she) come from... what a retard!" She turned white when she saw us in her line. I was furious, and ready to go to her supervisor. But my daughter asked me not to, and simply, flatly stated, "Don't worry about it. People talk about me like that all the time. They just don't know any better."

WHAT ADVICE OR WORDS OF ENCOURAGEMENT WOULD YOU GIVE TO GIRLS WITH AS?

Don't ever be embarrassed or ashamed of who you are. And just as important, try not to spend too much energy trying to be something you're not. You are a special gift from God to the world. It's easy to be "average" but it is a blessing to be unique.

WHAT ADVICE WOULD YOU GIVE TO PARENTS OF GIRLS WITH AS?

- Moms and Dads—*educate yourselves!!! Educate your family!!! Educate your child's teachers!!!* She can't do it, it's up to you.

- Don't expect your daughter to be you. Don't try to stamp your personality on her. She will be who she is, she won't morph into a replica of you. I think that's important.

- Never blame her, your spouse or yourself for her Asperger's. It is no one's fault, it's just the way it is.

- Don't let your feelings get hurt because of her need for solitude, she doesn't crave it as an escape from you, rather as a need to stop the world from spinning so fast and to survive in her own world.

- Be very careful of your advice to her. She will be very literal, and she will remember everything you say. Choose your words carefully and wisely.

- If you have other children, don't play favorites. That will only cause deep-rooted resentment.

- Love her for who she is, not for who you would like her to be. Enjoy the girl she is and the woman she becomes.

- You can discipline a nonautistic child using complex reasoning skills. You cannot discipline an autistic child in the same way, he/she would not understand complex reasoning skills. My daughter danced to a different drum than her nonautistic peers. We had to embrace her uniqueness and not squash her individualism. It did no good whatsoever to "punish" her for tantrums, or to "explain" things to her. She is wired differently and to expect the same rules/procedures to work for her would be futile.

- You are not alone. If needed, look for Asperger support groups in your community to help her and you cope with life's challenges. (Deborah)

APPENDIX

LIST OF FEMALE ASPERGER SYNDROME TRAITS

Appearance/personal habits	Intellectual/giftedness/ education/vocation	Emotional/physical	Social/relationships
Dresses comfortably due to sensory issues and practicality.	May have been diagnosed as autistic or Asperger's when young, or may have been thought of as gifted, shy, sensitive, etc. May also have had obvious or severe learning deficits.	Emotionally immature and emotionally sensitive.	Words and actions are often misunderstood by others.
Will not spend much time on grooming and hair. Hairstyles usually have to be "wash and wear." Can be quite happy not grooming at all at times.	Often musical, artistic.	Anxiety and fear are predominant emotions.	Perceived to be cold-natured and self-centered; unfriendly.
Eccentric personality; may be reflected in appearance.	May have a savant skill or strong talent(s).	More open to talking about feelings and emotional issues than males with AS.	Is very outspoken at times, may get very fired up when talking about passions/obsessive interests.
Is youthful for her age, in looks, dress, behavior and tastes.	May have a strong interest in computers, games, science, graphic design, inventing, things of a technological and visual nature.	Strong sensory issues—sounds, sights, smells, touch, and prone to overload. (Less likely to have taste/ food texture issues as males.)	Can be very shy or mute.
Usually a little more expressive in face and gesture than male counterparts.	More verbal thinkers may gravitate to writing, languages, cultural studies, psychology.	Moody and prone to bouts of depression. May have been diagnosed as bipolar or manic depressive (common comorbids of autism/AS) while the AS diagnosis was missed.	Like her male counterpart, will shut down in social situations once overloaded, but is generally better at socializing in small doses. May even give the appearance of skilled, but it is a "performance."
May have many androgynous traits despite an outwardly feminine appearance. Thinks of herself as half-male/half-female (well-balanced anima/animus).	May be a self-taught reader, have been hyperlexic as a child, and will possess a wide variety of other self-taught skills as well.	Probably given several different prescriptions to treat symptoms. Will be very sensitive to medications and anything else she puts in her body so may have had adverse reactions.	Doesn't go out much. Will prefer to go out with partner only or children if she has them.
May not have a strong sense of identity, and can be very chameleon-like, especially before diagnosis.	May be highly educated but will have had to struggle with social aspects of college. May have one or many partial degrees.		Will not have many girlfriends and will not do "girly" things like shopping with them or have get-togethers to "hang out."

Appearance/personal habits	Intellectual/giftedness/ education/vocation	Emotional/physical	Social/relationships
Enjoys reading and films as a retreat, often sci-fi, fantasy, children's, can have favorites which are a refuge.	Can be very passionate about a course of study or job, and then change direction or go completely cold on it very quickly.	Will have mild to severe gastro-intestinal difficulties—e.g. ulcers, acid reflux, IBS, etc.	Will have a close friend or friends in school, but not once adulthood is reached.
Uses control as a stress management technique: rules, discipline, rigid in certain habits, which will contradict her seeming unconventionality.	Will often have trouble holding onto a job and may find employment daunting.	Stims to soothe when sad or agitated: rocking, face-rubbing, humming, finger flicking, leg bouncing, finger- or foot-tapping, etc.	May or may not want to have a relationship. If she is in a relationship, she probably takes it very seriously but she may choose to remain celibate or alone.
Usually happiest at home or in other controlled environment.	Highly intelligent, yet sometimes can be slow to comprehend due to sensory and cognitive processing issues. Will not do well with verbal instruction—needs to write down or draw diagram.	Similarly physical when happy: hand flapping, clapping, singing, jumping, running around, dancing, bouncing. Prone to temper or crying meltdowns, even in public, sometimes over seemingly small things due to sensory or emotional overload.	Due to sensory issues, will either really enjoy sex or strongly dislike it.
	Will have obsessions but they are not as unusual as her male counterpart's (less likely to be a "trainspotter").	Hates injustice and hates to be misunderstood; this can incite anger and rage.	If she likes a male, she can be extremely, noticeably awkward in her attempts to let him know, e.g. she may stare when she sees him or call him repeatedly.
		Prone to mutism when stressed or upset, esp. after a meltdown. Less likely to stutter than male counterparts but may have raspy voice, monotone at times, when stressed or sad.	This is because she fixates and doesn't understand societal gender roles. This will change with maturity.
			Often prefers the company of animals but not always, due to sensory issues.

Will usually be very proud and protective of the gifts that Asperger's/autism has bestowed, but would like to be more at ease in the world and suffer less.

Rudy Simone 2009 © www.help4aspergers.com

Summary of Some Main Female/Male Differences

- Usually a little more expressive in face and gesture than male counterparts.

- Better at mirroring than males and so may mirror many different types of personalities. Hence females may not have a strong sense of identity, and can be very chameleon-like, especially before diagnosis.

- Will have obsessions but they are not as abstruse or unusual as her male counterpart's and tend to be more practical (less likely to be a "trainspotter").

- More open to talking about feelings and emotional issues than males with AS.

- Less likely to receive early, correct diagnosis because the criteria are based on male behaviors/traits. (Hans Asperger studied males only.) More likely to be diagnosed as bipolar or manic depressive (common comorbids of autism/AS).

- Physical gestures/behaviors when happy more expressive than males: hand flapping, clapping, singing, jumping up and down, running around, dancing, bouncing—this pertains to adult women as well as girls.

- Adult females are prone to both temper and crying meltdowns, even in public, sometimes over seemingly small things due to sensory or emotional overload. Hunger/food issues seem to be a common trigger. Adult males not prone to crying.

- Tends to receive less tolerance and more expectation from others, because she appears more adept.

- Like males, she will dress comfortably, but may be thought androgynous, as she may have an aversion to makeup and complicated hair and clothing styles.

- Less likely to stutter than male counterparts when stressed or upset; although both may have a raspy, choked, or monotone voice, or suffer mutism at those times.

- Females are generally better at socializing in small doses. May even give the appearance of skilled, but it is a "performance." Like her male counterpart, will shut down in social situations once overloaded.

- More likely to keep pets for emotional support but not always, due to sensory issues.

Rudy Simone 2009 © www.help4aspergers.com

References and Resources

Campbell-McBride, N. (2004) *Gut and Psychology Syndrome: Natural Treatment for Autism, ADD/ADHD, Dyslexia, Dyspraxia, Depression, Schizophrenia.* Cambridge: Medinform Publishing.

Carley, M.J. (2008) *Asperger's from the Inside Out.* New York: Penguin Books.

Edelson, S. (2009) *Autism, Puberty, and the Possibility of Seizures.* Together for Autism. Available at www.togetherforautism.org/articles/autism_puberty_and_seizures. php, accessed on 24 December 2009.

Gates, D. (2006) *The Body Ecology Diet*, 10th edn. Bogart, GA: Body Ecology.

Grandin, T. (2006) *Thinking in Pictures.* New York: Vintage.

Hayashi, M., Kato, M., Igarashi, K. and Kashima, H. (2008) "Superior fluid intelligence in children with Asperger's disorder." *Brain and Cognition 66*, 3, 306–310.

Hendrickx, S. (2009) *Asperger Syndrome and Employment: What People with Asperger Syndrome Really Really Want.* London: Jessica Kingsley Publishers.

Lawrence, R. (producer) and Næss, P. (director). (2005) *Mozart and the Whale* [motion picture]. United States: Big City Pictures. Based on the book by J. Newport, M. Newport and Dodd, J.

Markram, H., Rinaldi, T. and Markram, K. (2007) "The Intense World Syndrome – an alternative hypothesis for autism." *Frontiers in Neuroscience 1*, 1, 77–96.

Meyer, R. (2001) *Asperger Syndrome Employment Workbook.* London: Jessica Kingsley Publishers.

Simone, R. (2009) *22 Things a Woman Must Know If She Loves a Man with Asperger's Syndrome.* London: Jessica Kingsley Publishers.

Simone, R. (2010) *Asperger's on the Job.* Arlington, TX: Future Horizons Publishers.

Stillman, W. (2006) *Autism and the God Connection.* Naperville, IL: Sourcebooks.

Szasz, T. (2008) *Psychiatry: The Science of Lies.* Syracuse, NY: Syracuse University Press.

WEBSITES

www.help4aspergers.com
Rudy Simone's official website.

www.aspie.com
Offers visitors a variety of opportunities to connect with Liane Holliday Willey, EdD, Aspergirl extraordinaire, generous human being and internationally acclaimed speaker and author on the subject of Asperger syndrome. Articles addressing Aspie relationships; articles for parents, caregivers and teachers; lesson plans; poetry; a pet therapy blog; interesting articles from other sources; PowerPoint presentations, and a FAQ section.

www.autismhangout.com
News, videos, webinars and programs all about autism and Asperger syndrome. A marvelous resource passionately run by Craig Evans.

www.camillaconnolly.com
Camilla Connolly is a successful Australian artist living in the small town of Murwillumbah, northern NSW. She has held many solo and group exhibitions and her work is held in both private and public collections nationally. Camilla was formally diagnosed with Asperger's syndrome in 2009, and often lectures publicly on Asperger's syndrome and women and girls in Australia.

www.grasp.org
GRASP (The Global and Regional Asperger Syndrome Partnership)
666 Broadway, Suite 830
New York, NY 10012, USA
Tel. + 1 888 474 7277
Fax + 1 888 47 GRASP
Michael John Carley, Executive Director
info@grasp.org

www.templegrandin.com
The website of one of the original Aspergirls, a true pioneer and one of my favorite human beings. You must read one of her books and see her speak if you really want to understand the wondrous nature of Asperger's and autism.